MOMENTS

OF

PERSONAL DISCOVERY

RELIGION AND CIVILIZATION SERIES

MOMENTS
OF
PERSONAL DISCOVERY

EDITED BY

R. M. MacIver

LIEBER PROFESSOR EMERITUS OF POLITICAL PHILOSOPHY
AND SOCIOLOGY, COLUMBIA UNIVERSITY

KENNIKAT PRESS, INC./PORT WASHINGTON, N. Y.

THE INSTITUTE FOR RELIGIOUS AND SOCIAL STUDIES
MOMENTS OF PERSONAL DISCOVERY

Copyright 1952 By The Institute For Religious And Social Studies
Reissued 1969 By Kennikat Press
By arrangement with Harper & Row, Publishers, Incorporated

Library of Congress Catalog Card No: 68-26194
Manufactured in the United States of America

ESSAY AND GENERAL LITERATURE INDEX REPRINT SERIES

This volume is based on lectures given at The Institute for Religious and Social Studies of The Jewish Theological Seminary of America during the winter of 1951–1952. Each chapter in this volume represents solely the individual opinion of the author.

CONTENTS

Foreword   *R. M. MacIver*   ix

I.   What a Poem Did to Me   *Douglas Moore*   1

II.   Ants, Galaxies, and Men   *Harlow Shapley*   15

III.   The Neurosis Wears a Mask   *Lawrence S. Kubie*   27

IV.   Out of the Things I Read   *Margaret Mead*   37

V.   Persons, Places, and Things   *Paul Weiss*   47

VI.   The Road to Understanding   *Lyman Bryson*   61

VII.   The Sum of It All   *Joseph M. Proskauer*   75

VIII.   There Really Is a God   *Harry Emerson Fosdick*   83

IX.   How to Live Creatively as a Jew   *Mordecai M. Kaplan*   93

X.   A Philosopher Meditates on Discovery   *Richard McKeon*   105

XI.   Thinkers Who Influenced Me   *Harold Taylor*   133

XII.   Arnold Toynbee Kindles a Light   *Douglas Auchincloss*   145

XIII.   Sometimes a Miracle Happens   *W. G. Constable*   151

Contributors to "Moments of Personal Discovery"   161

Index   163

vii

PREFACE

Since its inception The Institute for Religious and Social Studies has been abundantly fortunate in the generosity with which distinguished speakers have answered its call. In the past year, for the luncheon addresses, being experimentally inclined, we besought from them a special and more personal contribution. We did so with a sense of temerity and no assurance that we were not unduly optimistic as well as importunate. We are all the more gratified by the response, the results of which are here presented to the reader.

It is one thing to ask an authority to talk on some subject within a field he has made his own. It is another to call on him to search, for our instruction and edification, his own memory of the way he has travelled until perchance he reaches back to some point, to some moment of experience, that brought him a clearer sense of direction and some vision of a goal toward which henceforth he must move. A number of our contributors have told us that the task we suggested to them lay quite outside their habit of thought.

The question we posed to them has been interpreted somewhat differently by different contributors. Some have given us the broader perspective of the formation of their philosophy of life. Some have taken us back more specifically to a conjuncture of their personal experience. Some have dwelt more on the impact of conditions that for them ruled out alternatives and determined the appointed path. Some have shown us more vividly a moment of discovery, the first glimpse of a new vision, as they listened to a teacher or heard the ringing words of a poet or withdrew to the "sessions of sweet silent thought." Some have found their inspiration in the circle of the hearth. Others have drawn it from a philosophical system or from a recognition of divinity or from the contemplation of galaxies and ants. But there is no end to the ways in which the inexhaustible nature of things finds particular access to the mind and heart of man.

Those who listened to the addresses found them of engrossing interest. In the printed form they should have no less appeal.

THE EDITOR

ix

MOMENTS
OF
PERSONAL DISCOVERY

I

WHAT A POEM DID TO ME

BY

DOUGLAS MOORE

This invitation is very risky because we all like to talk about ourselves, and the revelations that come from these talks might have a certain clinical significance. I am going to assume from the first that you will accept a theory that I have held that native art in America has always been regarded distrustfully. That is natural to any pioneer civilization. I will not say we are a pioneer civilization now. I think we are definitely emerging from it, but the pattern of American civilization for a long period was firmly resistant to the arts as a natural accompaniment to life.

Any artist believes in art as many other people believe in religion. The two things are not mutually exclusive, but art to the artist is a natural form of self-expression. The artist is a person who feels in his environment certain things that are moving and stirring, and essentially he seeks with his talents and with his training to present those for the enjoyment of his fellow men. That has always been the great value of the artist.

In the United States, when it came time for us to turn our attention to the arts, it was found that we had to look abroad for them, music, painting, poetry, all of an imported variety, and behind the idea of the validity of European art as opposed to native American art, were arrayed the forces of wealth, of fashion, of education.

The careers of many artists of the nineteenth century show this clearly. I can tell you of three men who were born within fifteen years of each other—Walt Whitman and Stephen Foster and Mark Twain. Every one of those men was a genuine American artist.

1

He felt American life keenly, but he found himself confronted by an attitude that did not regard American material as fit subject matter for art, and each one of them suffered from lack of appreciation and understanding.

Walt Whitman who now, after he was recognized in Europe, has been regarded as perhaps our greatest poet, was considered by his contemporaries vastly inferior to Longfellow, to Lowell, to Whittier, to the accepted poets of the period.

Stephen Foster who had a remarkable gift for melody that sounds American suffered from lack of training. It was not possible in this country at that time to develop those talents. If Stephen Foster were to appear today, the chances would be that he could have training to embody his inspiration in a perhaps more extended type of composition, but Stephen Foster was hardly appreciated at all in his time and died in the charity ward of the Bellevue Hospital.

Mark Twain, we know from *The Ordeal of Mark Twain* by Van Wyck Brooks, married a very respectable wife. Her name was Olivia Langdon, and she was the daughter of a coal merchant. Olivia Langdon hoped Mark Twain would always write the kind of things that people in Boston society thought were important and valid, that he should deal with classical subjects and so on. When he wrote *Huckleberry Finn,* which eventually was regarded by most people as his masterpiece, he had to do it more or less in secret so Olivia would not know what he was up to.

I was born into this American civilization in 1893, and my mother wanted me to study music, so I did, and I would have given it up if she had not been firm about it. I could not see why I should devote all that time to practice, and it seemed to me very unfair and unreasonable, but she thought it worthwhile, so I did, which is a tribute to American motherhood. But music to me at that time was European music, it was German music, it was French music, it was Italian music, it was Russian, but certainly not American. There was an American music, and I liked it, and I played it. It was ragtime, it was "coon" songs, it was something that represented an underworld, you might say, of American art because there always has been an American art, there has always been art which is the spontaneous expression of the individual to his environment, but it was, if you will, bootlegged art. The attitude of my teachers remained firm that nothing American could be worthy of serious study. McDowell was allowed because McDowell after all had had a successful German tour, and I believe he had studied with Reinberger, a perfectly authentic German composer. He brought back enough of German Romanticism to make his music denatured and possible to present to the serious American student of music.

At Yale where I studied music, Horatio Parker, who was trained in music also by Reinberger and followed the best traditions of German music, was in charge at that time. No one seemed to regard American music as of any importance at all.

Poetry and painting had gone ahead faster, and by this time we had some realization of the importance of American poetry. We had some realization of the stature of Whitman. Three poets came to Yale in succession. We met them at the Elizabethan Club. It was a place where undergraduates who were considered literary or artistic were permitted to meet great literary figures. The first one was Alfred Noyes. He charmed us. The second was William Butler Yeats, a poet's poet. He looked like a poet. He read like a poet. We thought it a strange phenomenon to hear Yeats read, but it definitely was respectable. The third person to be introduced—I did not hear him read—was an American poet, and could not possibly be any good. He was Vachel Lindsay. I do not know if many of you are familiar with Vachel Lindsay. We do not hear him discussed much today.

He was born in Springfield, Ohio, in 1879, and he had a strange notion of the importance of art in the life of the individual, so much so that he would devote his summers traveling around the country on vagabond trips. He would write poems, print them up, and stand on street corners and sell them to people. Somebody would come along and he would say, "Want to buy a poem? I have just written a poem." Can you imagine a thing like that happening in the United States? People thought he was a lunatic. He brought in this strange poetry that was almost like a football cheer. In fact, he calls some of his poems chants. He tells about the time when he went to speak at a university and they greeted him with a college yell and he replied with the poem, "Calliope": "I am some Kallyope, willy-wah, willy-wah, willy-wahoo." It sounds very much like a college cheer.

Well, Vachel Lindsay, we took one look at him and we recoiled in horror. He had the wrong kind of haircut. It was a haircut which we called in those days a fireman's haircut which consisted of shaving up to the beginning of the hair and letting the hair be quite thick there. He had ill-fitting clothes. He wore white socks. He did all the things that the Yale undergraduates regarded as improper. He seemed quite crude. He came right in and said he had a poem about how to pronounce his first name, and the line was: "My name rhymes with Rachel, it doesn't with satchel," I have forgotten what the other possibilities were. But anyway it was a dismal failure this encounter, and as I say, I did not hear him read, and he went out of my mind.

Some years later I was living in Cleveland and worked at the Art Museum there. Living in Cleveland was a sobering experience after the exciting times around New Haven and New York where one came in contact with literary figures, and so one day we were thrown into a great excitement by the librarian coming in and saying, "Guess who is in the library studying books on Egypt." It turned out to be Vachel Lindsay, so we said, "Oh, do ask him to come into the staff room and meet us all and talk with us."

So he came in and this time I was a little more mature and I found him stimulating and interesting. It was a sort of a lonesome life for an artist out there in Cleveland in those days and so I asked him—I said, "My wife is just coming back from the hospital. Our second daughter has just been born. My wife will be back next Wednesday, and I know that she would love to meet you. Won't you come and spend the evening with us?"

He was delighted. I suppose he found it rather lonesome out there, too. So he came to dinner and the three of us sat down and started talking about one subject and another, about America, and I found our points of view were quite different. Some things I regarded as being rather lamentable about our American civilization, for instance, the figure of P. T. Barnum always seemed to me vulgar. His strange career could not happen in Europe, and ranging from

Jennie Lind to General Tom Thumb, and the circus, it was not particularly attractive.

That sort of thing interested Lindsay very much, and I remember the talk got around to Bryan. I thought I was really on safe ground here with Bryan, and I said, "Well, he certainly is an awful figure, this William Jennings Bryan. He represents a kind of cheap oratory, his views are extremely unsound." Lindsay pricked up his ears and said, "Have you ever seen him?" I said, "No." He said, "Well, he used to get up on the platform, and the first thing he would do would be to stand there for a minute and he would begin to swell and swell and swell. They call him a damn fool, but how does he do that?"

So he offered to read us his poem on Bryan, and I am going to venture to read that poem to you today because I think that it changed my whole feeling and understanding about what it is to be an artist in the United States. It is a long poem, but it is a very interesting subject, and I hope you will bear with me because I am afraid that today not many people are reading Vachel Lindsay.

It is called: "Bryan, Bryan, Bryan, Bryan." [1]

Bryan, Bryan, Bryan, Bryan

The Campaign of Eighteen Ninety-six as Viewed at
the Time by a Sixteen-Year-Old, etc.

I

In a nation of one hundred fine, mob-hearted, lynching, relenting, re-
penting millions,
There are plenty of sweeping, swinging, stinging, gorgeous things to
shout about,
And knock your old blue devils out.

I brag and chant of Bryan, Bryan, Bryan,
Candidate for president who sketched a silver Zion,
The one American Poet who could sing outdoors,
He brought in tides of wonder, of unprecedented splendor,

[1] Vachel Lindsay, "Bryan, Bryan, Bryan, Bryan," *The Collected Poems of Vachel Lindsay*, The Macmillan Company, New York, 1941.

Wild roses from the plains, that made hearts tender,
All the funny circus silks
Of politics unfurled,
Bartlett pears of romance that were honey at the cores,
And torchlights down the street, to the end of the world.

There were truths eternal in the gab and tittle-tattle.
There were real heads broken in the fustian and the rattle.
There were real lines drawn:
Not the silver and the gold,
But Nebraska's cry went eastward against the dour and old,
The mean and cold.

It was eighteen ninety-six and I was just sixteen
And Altgeld ruled in Springfield, Illinois,
When there came from the sunset Nebraska's shout of joy:
In a coat like a deacon, in a black Stetson hat
He scourged the elephant plutocrats
With barbed wire from the Platte.
The scales dropped from their mighty eyes.
They saw that summer's noon
A tribe of wonders coming
To a marching tune.

Oh, the longhorns from Texas,
The jay hawks from Kansas,
The plop-eyed bungaroo and giant giassicus,
The varmin, chipmunk, bugaboo,
The horned-toad, prairie-dog and ballyhoo,
From all the newborn states arow,
Bidding the eagles of the west fly on,
Bidding the eagles of the west fly on.
The fawn, prodactyl and thing-a-ma-jig,
The rakaboor, the hellangone,
The whangdoodle, batfowl and pig,
The coyote, wild-cat and grizzly in a glow,
In a miracle of health and speed, the whole breed abreast,
They leaped the Mississippi, blue border of the West,
From the Gulf to Canada, two thousand miles long:—
Against the towns of Tubal Cain,

Ah,—sharp was their song.
Against the ways of Tubal Cain, too cunning for the young,
The longhorn calf, the buffalo and wampus gave tongue,

These creatures were defending things Mark Hanna never dreamed:
The moods of airy childhood that in desert dews gleamed,
The gossamers and whimsies
The monkeyshines and didoes
Rank and strange
Of the canyons and the range,
The ultimate fantastics
Of the far western slope,
And of prairie schooner children
Born beneath the stars,
Beneath falling snows,
Of the babies born at midnight
In the sod huts of lost hope,
With no physician there,
Except a Kansas prayer,
With the Indian raid a howling through the air.

And all these in their helpless days
By the dour East oppressed,
Mean paternalism
Making their mistakes for them,
Crucifying half the West,
Till the whole Atlantic coast
Seemed a giant spiders' nest.

And these children and their sons
At last rode through the cactus,
A cliff of mighty cowboys
On the lope,
With gun and rope.
And all the way to frightened Maine the old East heard them call,
And saw our Bryan by a mile lead the wall
Of men and whirling flowers and beasts,
The bard and the prophet of them all.
Prairie avenger, mountain lion,
Bryan, Bryan, Bryan, Bryan,

Gigantic troubadour, speaking life a siege gun,
Smashing Plymouth Rock with his boulders from the West,
And just a hundred miles behind, tornadoes piled across the sky,
Blotting out sun and moon,
A sign on high.

Headlong, dazed and blinking in the weird green light,
The scalawags made moan,
Afraid to fight.

II

When Bryan came to Springfield, and Altgeld gave him greeting,
Rochester was deserted, Divernon was deserted,
Mechanicsburg, Riverton, Chickenbristle, Cotton Hill,
Empty: for all Sangamon drove to the meeting—
In silver-decked racing cart,
Buggy, buckboard, carryall,
Carriage, phaeton, whatever would haul,
And silver-decked farm-wagons gritted, banged and rolled,
With the new tale of Bryan by the iron tires told.

The State House loomed afar,
A speck, a hive, a football,
A captive balloon!
And the town was all one spreading wing of bunting, plumes, and sun-
shine,
Every rag and flag, and Bryan picture sold,
When the rigs in many a dusty line
Jammed our streets at noon,
And joined the wild parade against the power of gold.

We roamed, we boys from High School
With mankind,
While Springfield gleamed,
Silk-lined.
Oh, Tom Dines, and Art Fitzgerald,
And the gangs that they could get!
I can hear them yelling yet.
Helping the incantation,

Defying aristocracy,
With every bridle gone,
Ridding the world of the low down mean,
Bidding the eagles of the West fly on,
Bidding the eagles of the West fly on,
We were bully, wild and woolly,
Never yet curried below the knees.
We saw flowers in the air,
Fair as the Pleiades, bright as Orion,
—Hopes of all mankind,
Made rare, resistless, thrice refined.
Oh, we bucks from every Springfield ward!
Colts of democracy—
Yet time-winds out of chaos from star-fields of the Lord.

The long parade rolled on. I stood by my best girl.
She was a cool young citizen, with wise and laughing eyes.
With my necktie by my ear, I was stepping on my dear,
But she kept like a pattern, without a shaken curl.

She wore in her hair a brave prairie rose.
Her gold chums cut her, for that was not the pose.
No Gibson Girl would wear it in that fresh way
But we were fairy Democrats, and this was our day.

The earth rocked like the ocean, the sidewalk was a deck.
The houses for the moment were lost in the wide wreck.
And the bands played strange and stranger music as they trailed
    along.
Against the ways of Tubal Cain,
Ah, sharp was their song!
The demons in the bricks, the demons in the grass,
The demons in the bank-vaults peered out to see us pass,
And the angels in the trees, the angels in the grass,
The angels in the flags, peered out to see us pass.
And the sidewalk was our chariot, and the flowers bloomed higher,
And the street turned to silver and the grass turned to fire,
And then it was but grass, and the town was there again,
A place for women and men.

III

Then we stood where we could see
Every band,
And the speaker's stand.
And Bryan took the platform.
And he was introduced.
And he lifted his hand
And cast a new spell.
Progressive silence fell
In Springfield,
In Illinois,
Around the world.
Then we heard these glacial boulders across the prairie roll:
"The people have a right to make their own mistakes. . . .
You shall not crucify mankind
Upon a cross of gold."

And everybody heard him—
In the streets and State House yard.
And everybody heard him
In Springfield,
In Illinois,
Around and around and around the world,
That danced upon its axis
And like a darling bronco whirled.

IV

July, August, suspense.
Wall Street lost to sense.
August, September, October,
More suspense,
And the whole East down like a wind-smashed fence.

Then Hanna to the rescue,
Hanna of Ohio,
Rallying the roller-tops,
Rallying the bucket-shops.
Threatening drouth and death,
Promising manna,

Rallying the trusts against the bawling flannelmouth;
Invading misers' cellars,
Tin-cans, socks,
Melting down the rocks,
Pouring out the long green to a million workers,
Spondulix by the mountain load, to stop each new tornado,
And beat the cheapskate, blatherskite,
Populistic, anarchistic,
Deacon—desperado.

V

Election night at midnight:
Boy Bryan's defeat.
Defeat of western silver.
Defeat of the wheat.
Victory of letterfiles
And plutocrats in miles
With dollar signs upon their coats,
Diamond watchchains on their vests
And spats on their feet.
Victory of custodians,
Plymouth Rock,
And all that inbred landlord stock.
Victory of the neat.
Defeat of the aspen groves of Colorado valleys,
The blue bells of the Rockies,
And blue bonnets of old Texas,
By the Pittsburg alleys.
Defeat of alfalfa and the Mariposa lily.
Defeat of the Pacific and the long Mississippi.
Defeat of the young by the old and silly
Defeat of tornadoes by the poison vats supreme.
Defeat of my boyhood, defeat of my dream.

VI

Where is McKinley, that respectable McKinley,
The man without an angle or a tangle,
Who soothed down the city man and soothed down the farmer,
The German, the Irish, the Southerner, the Northerner,

Who climbed every greasy pole, and slipped through every crack;
Who soothed down the gambling hall, the bar-room, the church,
The devil vote, the angel vote, the neutral vote,
The desperately wicked, and their victims on the rack,
The gold vote, the silver vote, the brass vote, the lead vote,
Every vote? . . .

Where is McKinley, Mark Hanna's McKinley,
His slave, his echo, his suit of clothes?
Gone to join the shadows, with the pomps of that time,
And the flame of that summer's prairie rose.

Where is Cleveland whom the Democratic platform
Read from the party in a glorious hour,
Gone to join the shadows with pitchfork Tillman,
And sledge-hammer Altgeld who wrecked his power.

Where is Hanna, bulldog Hanna.
Low-browed Hanna, who said: "Stand pat"?
Gone to his place with old Pierpont Morgan.
Gone somewhere . . . with lean rat Platt.

Where is Roosevelt, the young dude cowboy,
Who hated Bryan, then aped his way?
Gone to join the shadows with mighty Cromwell
And tall King Saul, till the Judgment day.

Where is Altgeld, brave as the truth,
Whose name the few still say with tears?
Gone to join the ironies with Old John Brown,
Whose fame rings loud for a thousand years.

Where is that boy, that Heaven-born Bryan,
That Homer Bryan, who sang from the West?
Gone to join the shadows with Altgeld the Eagle,
Where the kings and the slaves and the troubadours rest.

I cannot tell you the power of Vachel Lindsay in his reading.
It was simply extraordinary. Anybody who ever heard him found
that it was absolutely overwhelming. I cannot tell you what an impact

it had on me. Suddenly he had taken one of the figures that seemed to me perhaps the grubbiest of all and had made poetry out of him. It made him stand for something that could only be American. Nothing like that ever could happen in another country—that full color and character of Bryan and what he meant to this young boy.

And suddenly it seemed to me that here I was living in a civilization and I was completely unresponsive to it. I thought at once, now I must do a series of portraits of great Americans, and the Americans will be different, not universal heroes like Washington, Lincoln, and Jefferson, but people like Bryan and P. T. Barnum, figures who were really a part of our color, a part of our earth.

I started out reading about Barnum, and read several books, and he so fascinated me that I wrote a piece about him and called it the "Pageant of P. T. Barnum." There was a movement for each activity of Barnum so that it made a whole picture, a biography of Barnum. I never got around to Bryan, but the next subject was *Moby Dick* by a man who also had a completely unappreciated career, Herman Melville. Herman Melville was practically unknown at the time he died. It has only been in recent years that the value of *Moby Dick* has been appreciated. I discovered in the process of setting a part of this novel to music something that was so much a part of us, and so moving. And then with Stephen Benét who also was a great lover of everything American, I had the good fortune to collaborate on an opera based on his story, "The Devil and Daniel Webster." Daniel became a figure much more full of life and more realizable than those other great figures who had been reduced to textbook level.

Today you will find many people who say music is an international language, that we should not seek to write American music. We never had a real American music, and it seems a shame we should not at least have a try at it before we give it up. It is all right for the Germans to give up writing German music, because they have had a lot of it. The same for the Italians and French. But our civilization is just becoming aware of its possibilities. This is no time to give it up and write in a universal language. The universal language is described as that of the twelve tone row which is advocated by a tired Viennese composer, Arnold Schoenberg who used to write pure German Romanticism and found this twelve tone row as a means of escape.

It seems to me that denationalizing music is exactly like prescribing Esperanto for our poetry. Take away from poetry the color of the English language, let us write it in a new language that all mankind can enjoy. As language is so much a part of poetry, such an aim would be ridiculous.

It is interesting to see that in certain countries there are composers who are very great to their own people, but do not go beyond the borders. For instance, in Germany, there is Max Reger who is enormously admired, but we scarcely know him here. In France Fauré is tremendously beloved, but Fauré is a mystery to all other nations. In England, Sir Edward Elgar makes every English heart beat happily. Elgar means very little to us here.

Why can't we have a music of our own, and if it is universal music, fine, because some of our greatest music has been universal music. But I remember a statement of Paul Rosenfeld about the American composer, "Piled up about him is gorgeous stuff that he cannot use." Isn't it time that our composers did something about it?

I feel extremely grateful to Vachel Lindsay for having swept aside what perhaps was a little bit more than average snobbishness in my background. But I think it is characteristic of an attitude that still is quite prevalent in this country, an attitude of regarding our American subject matter as something inferior. I do not believe in jingoistic art. I believe one cannot write American music merely by setting the Gettysburg Address. It has got to be something that is part of one's experience, something that has entered into the very life of the artist, and then he should respond to it. It has been one of the imperishable heritages of the world, of mankind, that we have had the artist to see the world about him and to put it into permanent form so that it can be understood and enjoyed by all his fellow men.

II

ANTS, GALAXIES, AND MEN

BY

HARLOW SHAPLEY

"And then, from the plot of the positions of these globular clusters, projected on the galactic plane," I was explaining, "you can see this peculiar asymmetry—you can see this lopsided distribution, which probably means that—Good Heavens!"–oathed appropriately—"Good Heavens, it means that the center of the universe may be away off there in Sagittarius, tens-of-thousands of light-years away! Wonderful! Or is it?" I said to myself, and to the colleague who was referee-ing these researches that had just revealed that the distances of the globular clusters were astounding—greater distances than we had previously supposed to be sufficient to measure the diameter of the whole stellar universe. Now this onesided distribution confronted us, this evidence of a very distant center of our own stellar system, this growing realization that the heliocentric universe was passing as an interpretation of our place among the stars and that a strange sort of eccentric universe must replace it.

Then came an orienting thought, an elementary but belated con-cept: "Wonderful, yes; but I have put it wrong-end-to. I should not say that the center of our universe is so remote from us, so remote from the proud observers. No, I should say that it is the trivial ob-server that is far from the magnificent center! He is the peripheral, the ephemeral one. He is the incidental biological byproduct of water, soil, air, and sunlight. He is off in a cosmic corner, unknown to the billions of stars in that galactic center around which the hundred globular clusters move, and to which they pay gravitational homage.

"No, never again say seriously, 'lords of creation,' when referring to this planet's mankind. When the ego, by way of this phrase, tries inflation, just let it dwell on the hundred billion stars of the Milky Way, ponder the stellar bodies that are a billion times the size of our sun-star, consider the nebulae and the great clusters of galaxies, and the millions of centuries that planets revolved before man began to blink with primeval wonder, and began to ask himself questions about heaven's shining lights." Only a part of those thoughts developed immediately from the examination of the plot on the galactic plane. The research urge rose above the philosophic shock. Objectivity prevailed. "Let's now plot them on the Y-Z plane. Let's strengthen the analysis by measuring twice as many clusters. And then let's pick them to pieces one by one."

But when the distant center thus revealed itself, the forerunning shadow of the grim cosmic truth registered indelibly with the inquirer; the intimations of inconsequentiality, aroused by this plot on the galactic plane, have never vanished. It was for me a new world; a world that was playing a stupendous act, a great show with most of the action elsewhere, and I but a confused bystander, temporarily watching the action, making a few notes, pointing to a few of the more obvious facts.

With proper imagination, I could have realized that the shock-material for proper human orientation has always been with us; and some of the poets have reveled in their personal despondency. (The theologians, however, and most philosophers have been distinctly hard of hearing; the whispering cosmic messages are ignored, still mostly drowned out by the static of their artificial argument.)

Indeed we did not need the recent sidereal revelations to correct our vanity. Microscopically as well as macroscopically the sedatives for humble orientation have long been with us. The microscope shows sights, and incites ideas, that should put us in our place. But somehow our own physical bulk and muscular power, compared with individual electrons, cells, light quanta, and bacteria have protected our vanities. We feel superior to the swift little activities in phototube or mouse. They do not incite easy humility in the observer and interpreter. Mountains and elephants, however, produce some natural awe; and these confounding stars, these longtime intervals of paleontology, these millions of other planets around other stars, possibly with superior beings—such large scale handiworks of omnipotence trouble our self-esteem a great deal. They are deflationary. Years ago we did not like to give up the idea that Rome was the center of the world. Later we resisted (I am speaking here for the more educated primates)—we resisted in spirit and argument the shift of cosmic zeropoint from the earth to the sun. We had liked that geocentric theory of the universe, and the importance it gave us. The move of the center to the sun, and then the move far out through the bright stars of Sagittarius, as we shifted our world concept from the little peripheral solar system to the total material universe—these moves began to take the stuffiness out of us. We did not like it much. The shift is still uncomfortable to many humanists and others. Heaven knows, we cherish our stuffiness.

Before we expand this account of an Astronomical Moment and explain further the meaning of the distribution of globular clusters and the influence which that sketchy preliminary picture of the universe had on my own material and philosophic orientation, I should record that there have been other Moments. There have been other flashes that provided an humbling realization of the human animal's place in time and space; other somewhat shocking revelations of the brevity of his experience and triviality of his contributions. And also some happy turns when order appeared suddenly out of a tangled chaos. I would not have been so startled and bemused by these events if I had been a more diligent reader of the philosophies of past and present. Sir Isaac Watts put it neatly in a hymn:

> Great God! how infinite art thou!
> What worthless worms are we!

That sounds humble enough, rather impressively humble until one explores the biological antiquity of worms, their store of instincts, and their marvelously intricate structure; and then he is likely to agree with my friend Henry Norris Russell—"How frightfully complimentary to man!"

Let us look at some of these other Moments. There was a time of adjustment when after seven years of research with powerful instruments on globular star clusters—on their structure, relationships, stellar content—I realized that we were relatively more ignorant about globular star clusters than when I started my researches. I had added more to the unknown than to the known. A store of technical papers were written; but I could not catch up with the unfolding scheme. I found problems that we did not know were in existence; and even now, many years later, I remain chagrined that we are still ignorant, without even good leading hypotheses, concerning the origin, dynamics, and destiny of these great stellar systems. It was something of a jolt, I mean to say, to discover "How much th'unknown transcends the what we know," and feel that it will ever be so, unless there occur some rich and favorable mutation of the human intellect, unless there come about mutations for the wiser and for the more comprehending. With our present neural equipment we are not able to know everything about anything; and doubtless there are other vast fields of the partially knowable that we do not as yet know enough to be ignorant of.

It is all rather discouraging for an ambitious inquirer—that is, it is discouraging until he orients himself into a frame of rationality where to him it is the research as much as the findings that count in the progress of the human mind. It is the inquiring, the question, not the final reply. How suicidally dull it would be if we knew all the answers.

This orientation with respect to the limits of one's comprehension is a rather vague though disturbing operation. It is hard to accept the nearness of the limits on comprehension, or the brevity of human time. Time scales are as humbling as space measures.

The spanning of the geological ages came as a sudden vision to me one time while kneeling before the great god of Biological Evolution. The kneeling was on a sandy lot at the corner of Lake and East Orange Grove in Pasadena. The altar before me was a hole in the ground. Out of the hole emerged busy and beautiful individuals of a rich colony of the Harvester Ant. I had seen scores of these hereditary societies and had greatly admired their industry in harvesting and processing the wild barley. Also I had noticed with admiration their valor in their hopeless combat against the invading scourge of the Argentine ant. But this one nest was different. It housed ants that were different. Little spots or knots or feathery protuberances were glimpsed on the backs of about one half of these tidy and intense workers—and that spottiness should not happen! Ants are clean, forever primping and polishing their shiny chitinous surfaces. There should be no spots or stains.

In a dozen other neighboring nests of this same *Pogonomyrmex californicus* there were no such anatomic anomalies. No growths on the back of the thorax. Biology was here doing something special to a nest of fifteen hundred workers, who served an egg-laying monster-producing queen, unreachable far below the hard surface.

Some specimens from this particular nest had earlier been sent to the leading American authority, William Morton Wheeler of Harvard University. In verifying the identification of the species he wrote that three of the submitted specimens had tiny nodules on the mesothorax. The ants were, in fact, pterergates—a pretty name derived from the Greek for wing and workers. At that time in the myrmecological collections of the world only six pterergates were known— three collected from New York (Bronxville), one from England, one from Belgium, and one from Cuernavaca in Mexico. Four different species were represented.

There are about thirty-five hundred known species of ants (only one species of man!), and practically all of these live in social organizations. In their societies they show a remarkable diversity and complexity. Some societies are primitive—barely more than the simple family; others extraordinarily integrated, far beyond the development of human society. But the ants were not always social animals, with as now one small aristocratic fertile caste passing on the inheritance from one generation to the next, and another caste, comprising the overwhelming majority (the common ant), with its individuals sterile females that have little directly to do with the genetic development. There was a time when the forebears of the ants were like flies and grasshoppers—everybody was fertile and everybody for himself— no central colonial establishment; no statism; all in completely free enterprise.

In those ancient days (probably pretty far back in the Cenozoic era, some hundred million years ago or more) the forerunners of the ants all had wings, two pairs of wings, like the wasps whose ancient ancestors they probably had in common. That was long ago. But now, for the past forty or fifty million years, the common worker ant has been wingless and effectively sexless and totally dependent (with a few exceptions) on his own community for food and shelter. Society had been discovered, adopted, and developed for millions of years before men tried it.

All this elementary myrmecology is setting the stage for the Moment. I knelt before the hole in the ground, armed with the curious information from Harvard, and examined more closely the Harvesters, near the corner of Lake and East Orange Grove. For not only could I see at one glance more pterergates than in all the past had been reported by the ant men the world over, but I could see that many of these nodules on the mesothorax were not merely anatomical bumps, faint vestiges, but were actually miniature wings with veining, supporting ribs, and all that makes up the mature ant wings that the queen mother temporarily possesses and uses in her nuptial flight. Seven hundred and forty pterergates was my final census—a strange nest indeed, with about half of the population queer. These winged workers were in body structure and in work assignments entirely normal. A few of the pterergates were equipped with all four wings— miniature useless little wings—and as they busied themselves about the mouth of the nest, they looked like four-winged cherubim.

What is so surprising about this observation of worker ants with functionally useless little wings? Perhaps nothing very interesting or surprising to you; but to me the phenomenon was recognized as a throwback from our twentieth century of the Christian Era to the Cretaceous period of the Mesozoic Era. It was a sudden bridging back from the present over ten million generations, or more, of mother queens of *Pogonomyrmex californicus.* On my knees before this biotic altar I was suddenly in the age of the mighty reptiles, when the ants were yielding gradually their independence as individuals, abandoning their ability to fly, and adopting colonial advantages and restrictions. Before me was a living fossil society.

An occasional reversion of a single individual to a primitive type might pass as merely a biological curiosity—a sort of freak or monster in the myrmecological household. But the hundreds of pterergates in this one nest pointed to the persistence of our primitive inheritance; pointed back to our lowly origins, social as well as physiological. (In using the word, "our," I have in mind all of us social animals.) We could not simply say that something went wrong with one of the eggs and a freak was the result. It was more than that, and suggested a genetic turn toward social primitivism. Here was direct evidence of our linkage with the geological past—a sort of recapitulation of the societal development, much as the human foetus recapitulates the evolution of the human animal. Or so it seemed to me. To me it was a look at an embryological stage of a highly developed society. It incited, of course, analogical thinking. Here was a societal throwback after ten million generations; and man's society has existed for a few hundred at the most!

If fate and the warring Argentine ants had permitted the survival of that nest of *Pogonomyrmex* ants and if the cruel operations of natural selection had permitted the reestablishment of winged workers to survive in the fertile descendants of their mother, one might imagine that this ant society, after fifty million years of experience, would now tend toward the non-social family rites of the Mesozoic.

But that is mere fancy and bears little on the Moment when the first realization came that society—whether human or invertebrate—is still tied to the past, still infected with the manners of geologically ancient times.

The globular clusters had helped to locate man and his works in the space dimension. The Harvester Ants provided me, at least, with an orientation in time, and a vantage point from which to view the current evolutionary troubles of our multi-nation society. Our society has so wondrously developed that its members may now ponder and worry about their place in space and time, but it has not gone far enough to be free of throwbacks to the primitive. We are likely to revert to the totally savage, or even to the utterly and cravenly self-centered, forgetful of the profits of social living. When *we* throwback to the non-social, wings do not sprout; but our visages harden; smiles and sympathy are no more.

Notwithstanding the antiquity of the sciences of geometry and astronomy, the art of measuring the distances to stars with any pretense to accuracy or great depth is a development of the present century. The use of the surveyor's trigonometry, with the diameter of the earth's orbit as a base line, is simple in principle, but because of the large distances of the stars its use was long delayed until skilful operators, with good telescopes and modern photographic plates, solved the measurement difficulties. Even so, trigonometrical methods, used in various ways, have yielded distances only to those relatively few stars that are within a few hundred light-years of the observer.

In consequence of the limitations in their measuring methods, the astronomers had until recently little data to use in speculating about the size of the stellar universe. They also appear to have been little concerned with the dimensions of the universe, or of any section of the universe. They surmised that the naked eye and telescopic stars under study formed a system, with the sun at or near the center and its radius a few thousand light-years. Thomas Wright and Immanuel Kant recognized two centuries ago that the Milky Way is composed of stars and that the spiral nebulae might be other stellar systems, so far away that their individual stars could not be seen. The popular writers of the nineteenth century often spoke of external galaxies, with the intimation that the size of the over-all universe might be considerably more than heretofore surmised from considerations of the individual stars. But the professional astronomers, busy with many of the difficult technical details of sidereal exploration and measurement, were pretty content to hold to the heliocentric view of the stellar system. The nature and dimensions of the whole universe were left for speculators and philosophers to dream about.

Then came a rapid development, and the revelation in which I along with many others had the good fortune to take part, thanks to my association with large telescopes and my being completely free for research. We had a good time, both protagonists and critics, in developing a practical photometric way of getting at the distances of remote stars, freeing ourselves, except at the beginning, from the limitations of trigonometric techniques. We developed the period-luminosity relation for Cepheid variable stars, which are immense stellar bodies undergoing pulsations that cause periodic changes in their light. The story of the Cepheids is both long and well known. Here I need only say that these pulsating stars, that imitate the light variations of the star Delta in the constellation of Cepheus, are the most important giant stars in the sky. Not only do they through their pulsations give us a clue to their total luminosities and eventually to their distances and the distance of any group of stars with which they are associated, but they also give us suggestions as to the evolution of stellar bodies and the nature of the radiations from stellar surfaces. It is fortunate for us, and our knowledge of the universe, that these Cepheid variables are widely dispersed in various stellar systems in addition to the solar neighborhood and the Milky Way.

But enough of these astrophysical details. Building up the period-luminosity relation and applying it to find the distances of the globular star clusters was a rare excitement and stimulating. That was when Revelation began to enter my *Weltanschauung*. That was when I began to wonder if the universe-interpreting astronomer had not bitten off considerably more than he could chew and digest. He could in time handle the thousands of stars within a thousand light-years. But it became apparent, after two or three years of work on Cepheid variables in star clusters and elsewhere, that the universe was uncomfortably larger, and more populous and inscrutable than we had supposed—either that, or our methods and observations had trapped us into some fallacious deductions. There were indeed some fallacies and traps, chief of which was the then little recognized presence of much dust between the stars—dust and gas that absorb and scatter the stellar radiations and lead astronomers to erroneous values of brightness and distance.

But there was no major fallacy. There was no getting around the fact that the new techniques revealed, for example, that the great star cluster in Hercules was more than 30,000 light-years distant. Here was a distance greater than we had known about in our trigonometric and photometric work on the isolated stars. Here also was a measure of much time, for the light we were photographing was more than 30,000 years old. For much longer than man has been semi-civilized, the radiations we now see and photograph have been detached from the Hercules cluster and traveling in the cold intervening space.

Here was indeed raw material for cosmic cogitation. This light just now arriving from one of the nearest of the globular clusters has been speeding our way at the rate of some 11,000,000 miles a minute for three hundred centuries. Only during the last one-eighth of its journey were our historical civilizations born and matured, and most of them have had time to decay and vanish as the Herculean light nears the finish of its 180,000,000,000,000,000 mile journey. A very interesting concept indeed was provided by these measures of the Cepheid variables.

It took me some years to sort out the few scores of globular clusters from the other types of stellar organizations and to study their variables and their most luminous non-variable stars. Other observers made important contributions. Many distances were accurately measured; others estimated roughly. Finally came the time for assembling the material. It had already been noted that there are more clusters in the southern skies than in the north. That was an observation on the apparent distribution. Some could be relatively near, others very distant. Some could be close to our Milky Way band, and others far from it. We had to study the variable stars and use the period-luminosity yardstick to find where in space they are.

With the best distances we could obtain at that time we were able to plot the actual positions in space of many of these clusters. We could then place them on three separate two-dimensional diagrams. There would be plots on the X-Y plane, on the X-Z plane, and on the Y-Z plane. The first was the revealing plot. It showed the globular clusters projected on the plane of our own Milky Way—on the fundamental plane for stars and galaxies in modern cosmogony. This plot showed the globular clusters grouped rather smoothly around a point in the southern Milky Way. Such a symmetrical grouping could only mean that 30,000 or more light-years in that direction must lie a massive central nucleus which was the gravitational center of our disk-like Milky Way.

In retrospect it seems that we were slow to see that these plots had made a decisive change in our view of the stellar universe. But eventually the older idea that the sun is in or near the center of the stellar system was abandoned in favor of the belief that the sun is located in some sub-system of a great Galaxy, perhaps in one of its spiral arms. The observational data that had made us believe for the first decade or two of this century that we were near the center of things could just as easily be interpreted on the new scheme, in fact more easily after Lindblad and Oort established the rotation of our galaxy, and the effect of rotation on stellar motion.

The space positions of the globular clusters show that the nucleus of our galactic system is far away through the bright constellations of Scorpius, Sagittarius, and Ophiuchus. In an early study we placed the direction of the center near the junction of these three constellations of the southern Milky Way. The data were not very extensive, and it is therefore rather surprising and agreeable that the many subsequent researches, using other types of stars and clusters, have verified closely that original determination from the globular star clusters. In galactic coordinates, if you are interested, the longitude of the center is approximately 327°, latitude 0°; in equatorial coordinates it is in right ascension $17^h 30^m$, declination $-30°$.

From where we stand our Milky Way is a mess, with dense star clouds, dust clouds, and aggregations of gas confusing the picture. Also these various entities are in motion that is both systematically smooth and turbulent. Further, we on the rotating earth are in motion around the sun which is in motion with respect to the neighboring stars, which are participating with us in a long circulatory motion about the center of the galaxy. Afflicted with these complications we therefore cannot give a clear and conclusive description of the central nucleus, or a value of its distance that is correct within less than five percent. There is an uncertainty of ten percent or more in the measurement of our speed around the galactic center, or the duration of one revolution. For the time being we settle on a speed of some two hundred miles a second (for us and the neighboring stars), and a revolution time of two hundred million years. Finally we put the total mass of our great spiral galaxy at something like two hundred billion times the mass of our sun, which in turn is more than three hundred thousand times the mass of the earth.

All these superlatives are inserted without explanation or apology to indicate that we have, in studies of the universe, gone a long way since 1917 when we first gazed with some astonishment at the evidence that the center of our universe, of our own galaxy among the myriads of galaxies, is apparently more than thirty thousand light-years from the little but comfortable abode of "the lords of creation." When someone asks me now, "What are you doing for the good of the world?", I ask, "What do you mean 'world'?"

After the expansive measuring in our own galaxy, the astronomers confirmed the speculations of the eighteenth century philosophers and the nineteenth century popular writers that the innumerable spiral nebulae are indeed other galaxies of stars, the over-all system extending beyond the grasp of our most potent telescopes.

With the new measures of the dimensions in our own system, we quickly realized that the Metagalaxy—the galaxy of galaxies—could well be measured in units much larger than those that sufficed for the naked eye stars and even for the globular clusters. But once we had accustomed ourselves to the idea that the cluster distances are large, and our Milky Way galaxy enormous, it was not difficult to accept without further qualms the measures in the Metagalaxy, where we now use as the common unit of length not the mile or the earth-sun distance, or the light-year, but a mega-light-year, which is a million of those modest light-years each of 5,800,000,000,000 miles.

That is enough of this report on some Moments of Revelation. Experience with the distribution and time scale of stars and with the paleontological records tends to promote calmness with respect to current terrestrial matters. It tends also to enhance one's respect for the over-all evolutionary trends which include the birth and development of galaxies, the origin and rise of animal societies cosmically isolated on a peripheral planet, and the struggle by the human intellect to comprehend and take part in what is going on.

III

THE NEUROSIS WEARS A MASK

LAWRENCE S. KUBIE

Not long ago I was on a platform with a distinguished friend, Sidney Lovett, the Chaplain of Yale University. He was a lamb among the psychiatric wolves who were present. Yet he looked very happy. I could not quite understand this until he explained that for years the padres had been taking it on the chin, all the jokes being at their expense. "That never happens anymore," he said. "Now they are all on the psychiatrists and I have begun to enjoy life again."

I am somewhat overwhelmed at the task I have undertaken. It is a peculiarly difficult one to me because I have to try not merely to describe a phenomenon, the process of inner illumination as we encounter it in psychotherapy, but also to give you some idea of how we relate it to the process of religious revelation, and finally how we attempt to explain it, in so far as we have succeeded in advancing even any partial explanations.

I feel like that famous old French mathematician who was about to address the French Academy. He reached the podium, gazed around, and said, "I have changed my mind," and went home. Whenever I have bitten off more than I can chew, I feel that way; and that is how I feel at this moment. You know how it is. When you promise to give a talk like this you hope that your wisdom will somehow grow enough, so that by the time the fatal day comes, you may know enough to be able to talk about what you have promised to discuss.

Nonetheless, there is a deeper reason why I am here: a reason which goes back to the devout atmosphere of my childhood home, to my own concern with religious matters when I was young, and to the processes of change that went on in me whereby that early interest became channeled into the direction of general science, and from the start particularly in the direction of psychiatry. It was in the midst of my years as an undergraduate at Harvard that I decided that I was not going to be the lawyer that I had gone to college to become; but to study medicine so as to become a psychiatrist. There has never seemed to me to be any discontinuity in this sequence of events. The interest with which I had originally started as a youngster went through various transformations into a transitory interest in the law—I think largely because I was argumentative anyway—to concentrate finally on the field of activity which has occupied me ever since.

Undoubtedly certain youthful personality problems influenced my development in this direction, notably the uneasiness, self-consciousness, and confusion in human relationships which characterized my childhood and adolescence. There were also a certain number of facts about the world and the people around me which attracted my attention. Long before I had words with which to characterize those observations, they began to make a difference in my own purposes. I began to see that human personality as such contained enormously powerful forces: so that each individual human being shaped and molded his faith at least as much as his faith actively shaped and molded him. Furthermore, I observed that many different kinds of human beings become lawyers, artists, poets, scientists, and ministers of the gospel: and that among those who were devout, there were divergences in personalities as wide as those to be found among people without religious devotion. This made me realize that there must be forces at work in human nature which operated on some level other than the level of faith, forces which determined what men did with their faith, forces which human beings must learn to understand and to control if they were going to be able to make effective use of their own devoted feelings.

I had friends among different groups within the Jewish community, both Orthodox and Reform, because parts of my family with whom I had close personal ties were affiliated with both groups. Through other friends I saw a great deal of a large number of members of the Society of Friends, again both Orthodox and Reform, and so on through a broad variety of faiths and forms. And wherever I looked, I saw that each human being made of his faith what he had to, not by conscious voluntary choice, but by reason of some powerful inner forces which had the power to determine his behavior, his way of living and feeling and believing and preaching, his way of standing for what he believes; just as these same inner forces determined the quality of human relationships both in the home and out of it. This extraordinary variety of temperaments, and the power which these temperaments displayed, gradually made me realize that one cannot deal effectively with any aspect of life without taking unconscious psychological processes into account as well as the conscious forces which shape human personality. In turn this led me to a conviction that there were no short cuts, no easy formulas by which a human being could purge himself of dross, of the unwanted primitive elements in his own nature. All of my later training proved that this process of change involves man in a slow and difficult and painful toil.

As years went on those early primitive observations—partly on myself and partly on others—led to clinical studies and to the study of the techniques of psychotherapy by which the moments of discovery are achieved. Therefore, at this point I have to take time to describe some of the more technical aspects of this process. I will not go deeply into technical formulations, only far enough to make understandable a point of view in approaching this problem which is common to us all. It is worthwhile to do this, because so frequently the psychiatrist is misunderstood. Indeed, some religious teachers seem to believe that their goals and mine are dissimilar: whereas it is only in our paths to the goal and in our attitude to the obstacles in that path that we may differ.

I can summarize what I have to say by pointing out that what we have learned about human nature in these past fifty years is that in all human nature there is a universal masked neurotic component. This neurotic component in human nature occurs even in the most normal of us. It has its origins in our earliest years. Moreover these origins are linked to the development of those very capacities which are essential also to our highest endowment, *i.e.,* the capacity for thinking and feeling in symbolic terms. Without these there could be no art or literature or science or religion. Thus man's highest spiritual and cultural attainments and his neurotic ability to get into trouble, arise out of this same capacity to make abstractions and condensations from experience, and then to represent those abstractions and condensations in symbolic form. This capacity for symbolic psychic process is highly vulnerable, however, and starts getting in trouble quite early in life. When I say early, I mean almost as soon as the infant develops his first primitive language sounds. The human race is not yet wise enough to know how to cultivate the spiritually creative aspects of the symbolic process while avoiding the destructive neurotic distortions. Indeed, all of our hopes to discover a way to prevent the neurotic distortion of human personality depend upon our learning more about how this distortion of symbolic feeling and thinking occurs so early in life, and how to avoid it.

The ultimate goal of the psychiatrist is exactly the same as yours. This is something we have in common, namely, the goal of a good life. Also in the effort to achieve the good life the experience that is sought in psychiatry is precisely the experience which is sought in religion, *i.e.,* the experience of an essential inner change in the human personality, achieved through a succession of moments of deeply moving and often painful discovery of truths about oneself. This is always close to the process of conversion. It is what William James described many times in *The Varieties of Religious Experiences;* and it is something that we see repeatedly in any successful effort at psychotherapy. When psychotherapy succeeds, one watches subtle, deeply moving, slow increments of change in a personality, each marked by these cumulative moments of discovery. These go on step by step throughout the process of treatment. Sometimes they occur only after long periods of baffling frustration, in which one wanders through the wilderness, not unlike *Pilgrim's Progress* or Dante's *Inferno.* There may be long periods of struggle without any sign of change, taxing equally the courage and the patience of analyst and of patient; but it will be rewarded in the course of time, by those deeply moving moments of discovery and of consequent change to which I have referred.

Before coming to that, however, we must talk for a moment about the Devil. For the psychiatrist, of course, the devil is within us. He is the pride which makes everybody want to be freed from pain without paying the price of learning how to be a different kind of person. Everyone wants to get rid of his toothache; but no one wants to change. This is true both in the struggle for religious conversion and in that process of conversion which is an essential component in any deeply penetrating form of psychotherapy. Many a patient comes saying, "Yes, I would like to get rid of my painful symptoms, but I don't want to be different. Don't tamper with *me*." This is the stiff-necked, self-willed, self-proud quality against which every kind of spiritual growth has constantly to contend. Personally I believe it to be one of the obstacles to effective psychotherapy which we have not yet solved effectively.

I would like to stress the fact that here again we are on common grounds. We psychiatrists recognize that in order to get well the human being must change deeply, and that this means that he must first *want* to change; but that at the same time merely wanting to be different is not enough. It requires the humility of purpose plus a complex technique. Furthermore, we know that the technique is not enough without the humility of goal. Moreover, the psychiatrist recognizes that illness can distort even this spiritual humility, and that the need to change can be as misguided as is the stiff-necked resistance to changing, that we can be neurotically dissatisfied with things that are all right about us, just as we can be neurotically complacent over things that are all wrong. All of this arises, as I have indicated, because we bring forward from our earliest years something damaged in our personalities. Furthermore I want to stress that this happens universally, in every stratum of society. It happens under the most favorable as well as under the most unfavorable economic, cultural, educational, and spiritual circumstances. In other words, the problem that we are discussing here today is truly universal and has to do with the earliest formative steps in the development of human nature.

Again we have in common the recognition of the fact that man does not find it easy to achieve the good life. He can define the goal, more easily than he can reach it. As a matter of fact, the mere task of being a human being seems to be more than most of us are up to. The human race has not yet grown up to human stature; and in struggling with this basic problem we are struggling on common grounds; and with supplementary but not antithetical techniques.

I do not want to gloss over actual differences of opinion and feeling. These exist. For instance, the ancient issue of original sin comes up for thought. I am not going into that problem here, although if we are to be inclusive in our thinking we must recognize that it has to be considered. Whenever I consider that vexed problem, I turn back to St. Augustine with considerable comfort, because he was a really wise psychiatrist. You all know his famous saying that the innocence of childhood is due less to the purity of their hearts than to the weakness of their limbs. Freud himself could not have put it more succinctly. What psychiatry adds to that is the effort to discover why that is true and how to deal with it both preventively and curatively.

This issue confronted me recently in a moving, perplexing, and illuminating situation. I was visiting a school which does a magnificent job with youngsters who have gotten into serious trouble. At the end of the day I sat around with the director and the faculty of the school, and with the Protestant and Catholic chaplains. I showed them a psychiatric film called "Angry Boy." It was an accurate documentary. It showed a youngster who had gotten into trouble, and had done some stealing. It gave you a glimpse of his background, of how this arose, of the stormy inner rages which he was expressing and of the resentments and jealousies which played into his blind grabbing at things that he did not really need. Then it gave a glimpse of the process of therapy, condensed and simplified, yet as true as a picture of that kind can be.

In the end it was a happy little picture, and both young chaplains were much moved. More than one nose was blown surreptitiously; and the young Catholic priest was among those who felt its lesson most keenly. We proceeded to talk about some of the implications of the film for the therapeutic techniques of this particular school. Suddenly the Catholic chaplain turned to me and, with genuine perplexity and alarm and almost with some indignation, said: "But no one said anything about sin!"

I answered that this youngster was sick, that he acted out his sickness in a way which in our mores is sinful, and that certain manipulations helped him to unburden himself of feelings which had been inaccessible to him before, so that as time went on he no longer felt unhappy, no longer mean or full of rage and hate and envy and jealousy. Thereupon he had stopped stealing. True, nobody had said anything to him about sin. Yet the change that was evoked was precisely the change that we would be seeking for if we had first made him feel ashamed and sinful. The essential question is which is the surer and the more lasting road to the permanent change, which renders the Good Life attainable.

In other words, the same mountain had been climbed. I was not there to say which would always be the better way to climb that mountain. Nor was I ready to say that there is always only one good way to climb a mountain. Maybe there are some mountains that have to be climbed one way and other mountains that have to be climbed another way, and maybe what we have to do is to sit down together, to compare actual case notes, so as to find out how lasting is the change of heart in different kinds of disturbance of the human spirit when these changes of heart are achieved by the technical processes which comprise modern psychotherapy or by processes which are more familiar to us in religion.

Here again our goal is the same. Our areas of possible divergence are chiefly over the paths to that goal.

What then about the moments of discovery which come in the course of such therapy? I would stress first the fact that they usually come in small increments. You will understand, therefore, why I cannot talk to you about sudden moments of vast revelation. These do happen, but only rarely in our attack on these problems. We are accustomed to achieving change by inches. The struggles are long and painful: and it is amazing how frequently that moment of illumination concerns something which seems minute. Indeed, as soon as it is put into words, it may seem trite and banal, and obvious to everybody except to the patient.

Patients often become chagrined after describing to some friend the insight into themselves which they gained through weeks or months of painful struggle, insights which seemed to them to be extraordinary and surprising and profound, until the friend says, "Why, I could have told you that before you ever started. You did not have to go to a psychiatrist for all that time, spending all that money, just to discover that. I could have told you that before you ever started."

Of course the friend could have. The things that are wrong with us are often quite obvious to everybody around us. But what other people see in us is one thing; our ability to see ourselves as others see us is quite another. What the friend misses is the fact that the essential change which has happened is not just that the patient now understands that 2 and 2 make 4, but that certain inner blinders have disappeared, blinders which made it impossible for him to see the obvious and which have made him try to prove that 2 and 2 made 3 or 5 instead. It is the elimination of the blinders of distortions in vision, the badly refracted spiritual lenses, which is the essential process of therapy in psychiatry. The moving discoveries which then occur are usually due to the fact that suddenly the same individual can see the truth directly.

I think of a woman of destructive fury: a fury which shook her relationship to husband, child, and neighbors. With the elimination of certain of these inner blinders, it suddenly became clear that a wholly different person was hidden behind this façade of hostility and rage and hatred and meanness. This discovery occurred without any preaching to her that she must be different. The words in which she described her new insight indicated that subtle changes had occurred in all of the unconscious forces which had made her behave like one of the ancient furies, and which had made her always justify and rationalize and defend conduct which she had always known to be destructive.

The first man who ever taught me anything about psychotherapy was a very wise man, William Alanson White of Washington, then the head of the St. Elizabeth Hospital. He gave an informal lecture in the psychiatric clinic of the Johns Hopkins Hospital, where I was studying. In it he said, "You know, there is no use in telling a patient that 2 and 2 are 4. If he does not see that for himself, there must be some reason why he cannot see it. While you are talking to him he may be very polite and say, 'Yes, Doctor, I understand that 2 plus 2 make 4.' But the next day he is not going to agree so readily and two days later he will have forgotten that he ever agreed with you. When you discover with him *why* he has to believe that 2 and 2 are 3 or 5, you never need tell him that 2 and 2 are 4. His own direct sense will then be free to carry him to the truth."

There is in that fundamentally true statement a profound optimism about the human spirit. I emphasize this because psychiatry is accused so often of being pessimistic, when in fact it is quite the opposite. Its basic premise is that if you can eliminate the blind spots and the distorting lenses which we acquire early in life, then for the most part human beings will see truly for themselves.

It will be helpful to think of the different forms of psychotherapy as a spectrum. At one end is that form which consists of an effort to alter the environment in which people suffer, to lessen the external stresses which play on the patient. Here the tacit assumption is that it is the social milieu which is ill rather than the individual. Not infrequently this is true: and when it is the case, all such external aids are an important contribution to human welfare. To do this takes heart and skill and imagination and human sympathy. Much of the magnificent structure of psychiatric and medical social work is a formal implementation of this skill. Similarly the drive to reform in economics and in politics is infused with this same hope: namely, the hope that if you cure the social ills, individual ills will heal themselves. In fact when the situation is sick but not the man, this can actually happen: but there are many people whose illnesses are of such a nature that they persist in spite even of ideal external and environmental circumstances. When this is true, we psychiatrists have to attempt to change the individual himself. This can first be attempted by relatively superficial devices: you encourage him; you give him hope; you train him and educate him, and find him a new job; you give him the support of art and literature and music; you rest him with vacations; you argue with him, plead with him, try to gain his loyalty. You use every conscious intellectual and emotional force which can alter a human being's conscious feelings and allegiances, his conscious thinking and reasoning. A certain proportion of human beings receive great help from this. Yet there is still a residue which remains ill in spite of all such efforts. These men and women have to be helped through a deeper insight, an insight which penetrates below the surface to the unconscious forces which operate on them, unconscious forces which they cannot see for themselves, such as the unconscious fears, hatreds, rivalries, and envies which distort their behavior. With these patients, the psychiatrist adjusts his therapy to what he sees below the surface of the patient's conscious personality. He may or may not try to make the patient understand his own unconscious problems. Where the psychiatrist is not content to understand the patient's unconscious struggles, but asks the patient to achieve an equally unsparing insight into himself, we make as heroic a demand on the human spirit as can be made. This is always difficult to achieve; and the mere fact that it ever is attained, is a tribute to what the human spirit is capable of.

I do not know of anything which is more moving or dramatic or more humbling than to see the change that occurs in a human being whose insights have finally broken through all of the self-protective, self-defending barriers, all of the false fronts, behind which we begin to hide ourselves almost from the moment we start to talk. Now for the first time a man begins to see himself truly, with all of his frailties, all of his false gods, as he really is. Thereupon, and this is the encouraging part of it, as he begins to see himself truly, he begins also to see other people in the world around him more truly. Out of this grows an extraordinarily creative identification with the struggles of the human spirit toward a good life.

IV

OUT OF THE THINGS I READ

BY

MARGARET MEAD

When I was asked to contribute to this series, I liked the idea. It would be something pleasant to keep in the back of my mind for a couple of months, something one might think about when walking along the street, something to ruminate over, a focal point around which associations might gather. But when I really got down to the question of what I was going to say, I realized that the thing I had thought at first I wanted to discuss—how, when you try to look backward to find a moment in which your imagination has caught fire, you find a tiny spark that gets bigger and then gets to be a bonfire and then gets to be a book—did not really represent the way I wanted to look at this at all.

Instead, it seems useful at this point in the history of our understanding of thought to look at the earlier periods of one's life as a network of small paths, any one of which may later become a deeply trodden road, not because originally it was cut deeper than the others or because it followed a river bed originally or because some terrific event cut it so deep that everything else inevitably poured along it, but because one has gone back to it and gone over it again and again.

During the past fifty years, we have been the victims as well as the beneficiaries of a theory of psychology based so extensively on the exploration of individual trauma that it has lead us to think of human life as a series of events, each one of which is related to major conditioning events in childhood. If your father died when you were two years old, everything was fitted into the background of your having lost your father at two. Now, it may be the peculiar nature of trauma to be limiting, to define a road that is cut so deep that you cannot take any other. Presumably it may happen more often when one is dealing with trauma than with gifts so that childhood, instead of representing a network of alternative paths, must be seen as the occasion in which one road is so deeply cut that it becomes a rut into which the imagination sinks so inescapably that the future is limited to repetitive behavior.

I think the psychiatrists will agree that this is a fair description of the behavior of many of their patients; it is not necessarily, therefore, a fair description of the behavior of the whole human race. But influenced by psychiatric thinking, we have tended to treat those events in life which may be described as blessings in somewhat the same tone of voice that we use to speak about trauma.

What I thought I wanted to discuss after going back and thinking it over again is a little hard to put in a sentence or so, but it was essentially my conception of the responsibility of those—I don't quite like to say "intellectuals" because it is a word that for some people precludes the artists—but of the responsibility that belongs to anyone who cares about our arts and sciences and philosophies, about our whole artistic and intellectual and religious tradition. I wanted to talk about how that sense of responsibility was built, how paths that were originally very light became more heavily trodden as life went on. When I started to think back into my early childhood over this path, I found that the first thing that came to my mind was a book by a man named Coffin. It was called *The Story of Liberty,* and it was a violent anti-Catholic book written by some red hot Protestant a long time ago. I have not looked at it for a long, long time, and I think, on the whole, it was a very dangerous book. But it had exceedingly vivid titles to chapters, and one title was "The Man Who Preached After He Was Dead." That chapter was a description of the digging up of Wyclif's bones by the monks at Runnymede. They scattered his ashes in the brook, and still they could not stop him. And I think that gave me my first sense of how important a book could be and how important it was that books be written and how, if one wrote a book, one could preach after one was dead.

That was really my only association with Wyclif, the only book I remember reading about him, but when I was doing a little exploring for this talk, I remembered that in a class poem I had written in high school I had recited the names of practically everyone whose name could be fitted into a rather imperfect meter, virtually all the poets and saints and sages I could think of, so I thought I would go back and look at that list. There were quite a few people there whom I must have known almost nothing about beyond their names—Petrarch, for example. The theme of the poem was the tradition we were all heir to, and there in the middle of this list, still surviving along with Dante, Virgil, Joan of Arc, and Sappho, was Wyclif. He did not "belong." If anyone had looked at the list from the standpoint of content analysis, he would have said, "Wyclif doesn't belong in this list." But he stood for a particular point about the way tradition was passed on, for the strength, the abidingness of the written word.

For the last lines of this class poem, which was at once deeply felt and very conventional, I had written:

> On your shoulders falls their mantle
>   Settling light as a caress;
> Will you answer, heirs of ages?
> 'Saints and Sages—we say *yes!*'

That has an unmistakable echo of "And departing leave behind us, footprints on the sands of time." It also, however, contained an image so curious that I thought it worth exploring. Where had I got the notion that the burden that was to be taken so seriously was light? After all, young people graduating from high school in 1918 had plenty of Longfellow in their ears, not to mention "The Lost Leader" that my mother used to recite with such feeling.[1] It did not really seem as if the burden should be so light.

---

[1] In preparing this talk for publication, I considered whether to include the two lines my mother used to quote:

> Just for a handful of silver he left us,
> Just for a riband to stick in his coat—

and I went back to the text of Browning's poem about Wordsworth to check the quotation. My inclusion of the reference to "The Lost Leader" was a spontaneous

The line, "Settling light as a caress," puzzled me enough to set me on a pursuit of the underlying imagery, and I decided that the lightness, as associated with a sense of tradition, went back to a poem by Stevenson that everybody here knows because it is the heritage of all properly brought up English-speaking children in every part of the world. It is this one:

> Dark brown is the river,
>   Golden is the sand;
> It flows along forever
>   With trees on either hand.
>
> Green leaves a-floating,
>   Castles on the foam,
> Boats of mine a-boating—
>   Where will all come home?
>
> On goes the river
>   And out past the mill,
> Away down the valley,
>   Away down the hill.

------

afterthought as I was talking. I had not considered it as I was preparing for this talk. To my great surprise, for I could not have quoted on demand any other lines of the poem, I found the prefiguration of the way in which I had invoked the names of the great in my old class poem, written in 1918:

> Shakespeare was of us, Milton was for us,
> Burns, Shelley were with us,—they watch from their graves!

and a prefiguration of my use in this talk of the image of the pathway:

> Blot out his name then, record one lost soul more,
> One task more declined, one more footpath untrod.

And then I remembered some verses I had written long ago as a Valentine for someone I admired very much:

> I've wandered in small sunlit paths
> Where you proudly would not look.
> I can only pluck you daisies
> On a cowpath you never took.

To my surprise, it showed even then an interest in the image of the little unimportant paths.

So we build up a "landscape of the spirit," where our eyes can wander, half attentive, many times before final choices are made as to which images to include in any finished picture.

> Away down the river,
>   A hundred miles or more,
> Other little children
>   Shall bring my boats ashore.

When I tried to remember all of this, I found I could not reconstruct the second stanza, although it is the images of this second stanza—the boats that were only light green leaves, the castles not in sand but "on the foam"—that were crucial. For it was the great fragility of tradition, coupled with the certainty that, nevertheless:

> Away down the river,
>   A hundred miles or more,
> Other little children
>   Shall bring my boats ashore,

which remained in my mind to lighten the load on our shoulders when, as an adolescent, I was calling on my classmates to respond to it with such excessive responsibility.

Then, when I tried going back again to another early path, I found two biblical themes which I think were important. The first was the parable of the talents and the exceedingly wicked man who wrapped his one talent up in a napkin and did nothing about it except bring it out again. At the time I heard that story, the pun on the word *talent* was more important to me than the more unusual meaning of the word as money. I came from the kind of family that scarcely mentioned even taxes, except to say that they were not heavy enough to improve the schools as they ought to be improved, so it never occurred to me to dwell on the literal point of the parable—getting a return on money. I put people who did not use money responsibly and people who did not use their abilities to sing and write books, together as people who put their talents in napkins.[2] It does not worry a child much to handle concrete images fluidly. I simply got the idea that the man who, having only one talent, had left it in a napkin and had done nothing further about it had done something very wrong. Whether the parable was read to me at home with special emphasis,

---

[2] The actual images are, of course: "I was afraid and went and hid thy talent in the earth" (Matthew XXV, 25), and "Lord, behold, here is thy pound, which I have kept laid up in a napkin" (Luke XIX, 20).

or whether I heard it from a pulpit on a day when a particular preacher felt very strongly about it, I do not know. But I got the idea that the sin that man had committed with his one talent was one of the worst sins I had ever heard of. And it got linked up with the sin against the Holy Ghost, the unforgivable sin that no one could explain to you and that you might commit, therefore, no matter how good you were. Together, these ideas—the sin against the Holy Ghost, and the sin of hiding your talent as the man in the parable had done—provided the religious setting for my sense of commitment.

I began to realize later that not only was I feeling after the obligation that was laid on each individual to use whatever gifts he had—to be very, very certain which they were and to use them wisely—but that also I was still preoccupied with the precariousness of human tradition. The Wyclif story is the story of the sturdiness of tradition, of how words once written will still survive though they be burned and though the ashes of the man who wrote them be scattered in a running brook. But the Stevenson poem still haunted me with the possibility that some day on some river those boats might *not* be brought ashore.

There was a play on the New York stage, about 1922 I should say, called *The Inheritors,* in which an old grandmother, speaking from pioneer days, describes an occasion when the whole family was away from home and another pioneer family, passing by in a covered wagon, stopped over as people did in those days when they found an empty house. They lived in the house for two or three days and went away again without ever having been seen by the people whose unwitting guests they had been. And the old grandmother said something like this: "And she baked a loaf of brown bread and left it there, and it didn't taste like any bread I'd ever eaten. They must have been some kind of foreign people who had a recipe that was different from any one we ever had. I used to experiment and try to make that loaf of bread, but I never could. I always hoped some day I'd meet that woman and she'd tell me how." [3]

[3] Susan Glaspell, *The Inheritors,* Small, Maynard & Company, Inc., Boston, 1921, Act I, p. 10.

And that play was one of a small set of impressions that added another element to the picture of the fragility of our human tradition—how it depends so closely on the effect of one human being on another. It is not only that books live, even though their authors may have been burned; it is also that if the right people do not meet the right other people at the right time the secret of baking the bread may be lost. Because it is not enough to eat the bread. You have to meet the woman who knows how to make it.

That particular path was cut deeper when I read the introduction to one of Malinowski's books.[4] Malinowski described his despair when, as a young student in Crakow, he was told he was not going to be allowed to study mathematics (I think partly because of the condition of his eyes). Coming out from his despair, he hit upon *The Golden Bough,* and, reading it, got a new image of what he could do with his life and what kind of scientist he wanted to become.

Again the shift from the person to the book. And the awareness of the shifting back and forth between the responsibility to maintain intact the tradition that has been set down in books, in pictures, in other permanent records, and the responsibility to preserve those human traditions that are carried only in human lives and human attitudes, became again intensified.

Of course, what I do in my own work by choice is to study the cultures of those people who have no writing and only the most rudimentary art, not an art that will delineate a culture to people who depend upon fine art as a principal bearer of culture. The culture of such primitive peoples perishes forever unless the human beings themselves are studied by someone outside their culture. So when I reached the end of my college course and it was a question of choices as to what sort of endeavor I wanted to pursue, the thing that was decisive was the picture Franz Boas and Ruth Benedict drew of the perishing small cultures on the edges of the world. They were unrepeatable, precious records of what human beings could do if they had not done something else. They were islanded away from the main stream of tradition and would never be repeatable. Once they were lost, we would have no record of them.

---

[4] Bronislaw Malinowski, *Myth in Primitive Psychology,* Norton, New York, 1926.

And at just about that time, I read a book by Mrs. Scoresby Routledge, who had taken an expedition to Easter Island.[5] This is such a tiny island that even in the 1930's the officers of a French ship with all modern navigation aids reported they had sailed over the site of Easter Island and the island was not there. However, the Polynesians had reached it twice with their outrigger canoes and had built strange statues on it that puzzled people very much. Mrs. Routledge reached the island with great difficulty, to find the last man who was said to be able to interpret the legends on the backs of the statues too ill to be of much assistance to the expedition. Two weeks later he died.

Here all these themes came together. There were marks on the backs of the statues to stand for the writing human beings might do about what they observed other human beings did with their lives. And here again was the complete fragility—the single human being and the ship that arrived too late.

Because the point I want to emphasize is the significance of oral communication, I should like to end with a rather complicated story, which started a year before Edmond Taylor published *Richer by Asia*. When he first came back from Asia we had a long argumentative luncheon conversation, colored by our mutual oppressive sense of the danger hanging over the world as a result of the new atomic discoveries. Both of us feared that civilization might be wiped out entirely, but he was, I think, more pessimistic than I. During this conversation I used the figure of speech of the time when men, having just learned to keep fire but not how to kindle it, held—perhaps—the whole future of the human race in their hands. It was even possible to conceive, I said, that at some remote period in time, one man—the man who sat up to tend the fire—might have held in his keeping the lives of the only human beings who had survived. And I suggested that at no other time in the whole of human history had the continuation of civilization been in such a precarious position, so dependent upon what the men of one generation might do.

Edmond Taylor was on his way to Canada to write his book, and I

[5] Mrs. Scoresby Routledge, *The Mystery of Easter Island,* Sifton, Praed, London, 1919.

did not see him again for a year. Then he passed through New York one evening and stopped over to read us a chapter of his completed manuscript—the chapter called "Mission to Morning." It is a very long chapter, the most beautiful chapter of a beautiful book. It is a chapter about a flight between the end of the war and the beginning of peace, from Burma to Siam, about looking down and seeing fires men had lit in the depths below, and about a decision that saved many men's lives, which Edmond Taylor attributed, together with his sense of the significance of the flight itself, to another book, *Wind, Sand and Stars*. When he finished the chapter, I said, "It's hard to know what to say, because it's so close to everything that I care most about in the world." And he said, "But of course. Don't you remember we talked about all this at luncheon a year ago?" But at that lunch I had not talked about all the things I have talked about today, only about the single image of the tended flame and the responsibility of each individual, according to his or her single talent, to keep that flame alight. Yet in the chapter Edmond Taylor had written, it was all there, beautifully reconstituted, said far better than I could have said it myself.

For he had written:

Whatever is made by man is the incarnation of human experience, and the reincarnation of earlier human experience. Because a man is gentle with a woman or a woman kind to a man, a child may be born who will be lighted by a glow of gentleness and kindness, and this light will be transmitted to other children, to many children, for children are made in many ways, and may be many things—a song may be a child, or a gentle law, or a kindly treaty, or a mathematical formula expressing the tenderness of figures, an idea that will become a machine, expressing the tenderness of cogs and levers, before it becomes again an idea and then an emotion, again a child of someone's flesh, expressing the love of man and woman.[6]

[6] Edmond Taylor, *Richer by Asia*, Houghton Mifflin Company, Boston, 1947, p. 334.

V

PERSONS, PLACES, AND THINGS

BY

PAUL WEISS

I

Everywhere we confront mystery too deep for any one of us to probe to the very bottom. Whatever is, is in part outside our reach; it seems to be, at least to some degree, alien to our spirit. All the rest of the world stands at a distance from us, defiant, insistent, obstinate. The things about us go at their own rates, not ours. They pursue their own careers, often blocking our efforts and intruding on us. We men are not entirely at home here, and never become fully so.

Some things, to be sure, play but a minor role either with respect to us or to the whole of things. Very few have enough value, or are obtrusive enough to make us, in the normal course of events, aware that we understand only snatches of the language of the world in which we live. For the most part we are content with what we may have happened to grasp. We see little to remark upon, in part because we are ignorant of ourselves and others. Both ourselves and others are possible sources of wonder, places from which the imagination can take its start and to which it must eventually return. Full justice is done to things only if they are taken to be occasions both for delight and perplexity, at once wondrous to contemplate and provocative of inquiry. Everything, in short, has the power to shock and to teach; each encompasses a secret whose nature is partly revealed and partly belied by what it says to the passing glance. To uncover that secret we must engage in a complex art of exploration. This art is best pursued by being divided into the art of resolute inquiry and the art of creative wonder, and then reconstituted in the form of a unified method by means of which we can at least in part master ourselves and the world. In adolescence most of us practice this complex art of exploration without having first distinguished its essential components. We are confused because we have not learned how to distinguish inquiry and speculation. In my own case the confusion lasted until I was past twenty-one. It would undoubtedly have continued longer had I not been rescued by friends and teachers.

I had left school when I was about sixteen. I was without focus, without money, having learned little and been inspired less by the subjects offered in a commercial high school. For some six barren years I occupied a dozen minor posts in minor businesses. During that time I read voraciously in a rather undisciplined way, buying and studying a wild miscellany of books on life and death, nature, science, logic, poetry, becoming no clearer, wiser, or even better focussed in the process. Somehow though, I hit on the idea that since proverbs epitomized the wisdom of the race I could come closer to the bone of truth by reflecting on proverbs. I remember hurrying to the library after the day's work was done, pulling down large collections of proverbs, and then reading and studying them until the library closed. In a way the proverbs satisfied me. They had an air of sufficiency, of finality, of bedrock, and seemed to turn everything else into a derivative or commentary. They also left me discontent. It was startling and dismaying to find that every list contained contradictory observations, all apparently equally sage and sound.

Still restless, vaguely searching for something I did not know how to name or to recognize, I spoke one day with a Japanese salesman who worked for the same firm. With some hesitation I told him of the things I had read and had been bewilderedly thinking about. With a confidence that awakened mine, he told me that I was interested in philosophy.

To think, during that period, was to act. Without delay I enrolled for philosophy courses in the evening session of City College. To the surprise of the registrar I enrolled for three courses of philosophy, to be taken at successive hours three times a week. I was in class from seven to ten. After that I rode home on the subway. The ride took over an hour giving me time to read my next assignments and other things. I remember being quite sleepy when I set off to work the next day; I believe my office work was found to be increasingly unsatisfactory. But I did not mind; I had found what I was looking for. I was then twenty-two.

City College at night was, at that time, a depressing place, even for one imbued, as so many were, with a passion to know. Tired, earnest, anxious men and women, after a hard day's work, came together in badly lit rooms to hear incidental remarks uttered by weary instructors. The classes were so large, the membership so fluid, the texts so inadequate, the attention so flagging, that it is surprising that any one of us learned enough to pass the examinations or had the energy to write the required essays. I had the good fortune, however, of encountering in two of the classes, Eliseo Vivas, now professor of philosophy at Northwestern University, at that time an eager, energetic, excitable, and exciting student. We two were somewhat violent defenders of opposite, partial truths which we hurled at one another with fury, to the delight of John Pickett Turner, our teacher, and to the surprise or annoyance of the other students. I think we were quite trying, though for the most part we were oblivious of the effect we were making or of the fact that we were taking up so much of the class time and the teacher's attention.

An existentialist before the day when such an outlook had attained the stature of a movement or the glory of a name, Vivas lived its theories with conviction and insight. It was from him that I, analytic, abstract, rudderless, first learned to appreciate modern developments in art and literature, and took account of the value and penetrative power of genuine emotion. The world has a complexity of which we have a dim awareness from the very beginning; we need the help of others to become alive to the nature of facets which are hidden from our sight. If we are fortunate, as I was then, the help comes at a time when it is desperately needed. We are, at such a time, told what things look like from a different angle, and how we can say what we believe with more sincerity and courage.

During this period I was at once excited and abstracted, avid for knowledge yet incredibly dogmatic, at once willing to study and unwilling to keep quiet and listen—faults which pursue me until today. I wrote constantly, though somewhat disconnectedly, interspersing time at the typewriter with reading of every kind. At City College there was a small prize offered for an essay written in a course during the year. The contest was open to students in the evening and day sessions. Apparently no one in the evening had yet found the leisure or the need to enter the competition. I did. The novelty of the entry was a factor in the decision to have me share the prize with Milton Steinberg. At the end of the year, without too much conviction, my instructor suggested to me that I ought to become a day student.

It did not occur to me until much later that this was a casual remark. It was enough, though, to prompt me to give up my job and enroll in the day session of City College. I soon found that all I had to do was to rent an inexpensive room, earn my food and rent by teaching English to foreigners and children some half-dozen hours a week, and I could spend the rest of the time studying, writing, and discussing. It is easier now than it was for me then to understand the astonishment of John Pickett Turner when he found that I had followed his advice and entered the day session, and particularly that I had decided to begin by taking a course with Morris R. Cohen.

I had heard but little of Cohen by then. And I did not know that his logic class was the meeting ground of seniors who, with considerable justification, prided themselves on being quicker, abler, and better read than the others. All I knew was that I had read Mill's *Logic* during the summer and had been much impressed with it. I wanted to find out more. I did.

Cohen was a remarkable man, in the multiple senses of that term. In appearance and in personality he was unforgettable. Frail, carelessly dressed, he had an enormous domelike head, quick alert eyes, a sharp angular nose, a lean, incisive, mobile mouth, and a jutting jaw. The figure answered to the person. Iconoclastic, clear-eyed, intellectually sure-footed, liberal in temper, quick as lightning, with an amazing amount of information at his finger tips, Cohen was the master of all the students he encountered. He offered his material and his arguments with great incisiveness, conviction, and compelling power, making him always to be watched, sometimes to be copied, perhaps even feared. He enjoyed intellectual debate; he sought clarity and definiteness, no matter what the dogma or the belief.

Cohen taught us to challenge, to try to be informed, to inquire. He communicated to us a respect for learning and ideas and trained us in the art of careful thinking. He gave us a sense of the value and difficulty of the intellectual life and showed us how to honor without servility the masters of it who had lived before.

Cohen made you feel that knowledge and perhaps the professorial chair gave a power not matched in force or dignity by kings or tyrants, for it took possession not of men's bodies or property but of their infinitely more precious souls and minds. These are genuine achievements, the mark of a great teacher. That is why his classes stood out above all others, places where young men gathered to be shocked, stimulated, disillusioned, disciplined, and redirected—and also I must confess, to see one another discomfited. One was sure in every class to find Cohen's reason, knowledge, and presence to the fore, supporting one another. He dispelled fallacies, overcame superstition and prejudice, sharpened wits, and made one more critical and intellectually self-aware. He taught—more by example and criticism than by doctrine—that he who did not think clearly, he who did not know, fell regrettably short. He offered a high standard by which we could justly judge ourselves, our contemporaries and all those who appeared in the role of philosopher. His fundamental guide was the principle of polarity, which enabled him to recognize the complexity of problems, to see the onesidedness of extreme views and to take account both of the defenders and the attackers of some basic thesis.

A critical intellect, such as Cohen's, even when backed with a sweet kindness which came to expression again and again through the interstices of his sharp dialectic, awakens respect and admiration. Even awe. It teaches one that every reality, no matter how important and respectable, can be a datum for an investigation, and must, if it is to remain worthy of respect and attention, withstand the biting effect of disciplined, searching inquiry. But the critical mind has little time for creative wonder, and can give no occasion for it. It quickens thought but tends to stop the imagination. In my own case Cohen had this effect. But in compensation he stimulated my appetite for the study of logic, and above all aroused my interest in two men somewhat unknown at the time, one living, the other dead, Alfred North Whitehead and Charles Saunders Peirce.

After graduation from City College I hurried off to Harvard with seventy-five dollars and a desire to study with Whitehead. By tutoring undergraduates, it was possible for me to get through the year just ahead of the bills. But all that was incidental. My eyes and mind were elsewhere. I had encountered greatness.

Whitehead was a man unlike any I had ever met. Rosy-cheeked, with unbelievably vivid blue eyes, courteous, gentle, above all eminently civilized, probing, perpetually ruminating, Whitehead was singularly uninterested in argument or dispute, with making himself personally evident, with a need to defeat or overcome. Our first meetings were almost comedies of error and frustration. Though his enunciation was precise, his speech crystal clear and his language simple, I literally could not grasp a single word in the hundreds he uttered the first day I came to his class. His British speech was beyond my grasp. He told me later that when he first spoke with me he could not understand a word I said. He had never heard an East Side New York accent, such rapid speech, with so many of the endings of words blurred or omitted. He had been in this country only three years then, and never had had the occasion to hear anyone talk about ideas in such a language or with such a manner. But he never let on. He was kindness itself. I learned about it much later when teacher became teacher and friend.

To listen to Whitehead was to be challenged not only in idea but in spirit and in value; it was to feel oneself tested not by him but by absolute standards of integrity. Rarely did he speak directly in answer to a question. Rarely did he stay with any topic for a length of time. His way was that of half-sentences, not altogether clear, but each adding something to its predecessor, until an insight, having no evident bearing on the remarks he had previously made, would stand out in sudden light. What he said was frequently subtler and more profound than a direct answer to one's questions could have been. I used to come home after an evening with him somewhat beside myself with excitement, carrying on a train of thought which more likely than not had little to do with what he had remarked, but which had been stirred and awakened by his insight and creativity. I would visit him years after when I should presumably have grown in knowledge, surety, and wisdom only to find myself still a screechy chalk mark writing trivialities on an uncleaned blackboard.

Whitehead still remains to me, after almost all others have faded, a man of genius, with a freshness and daring matched nowhere else. He was radically honest with himself and others, simple without naïveté, perceptively unafraid of the commonplace and obtrusive, courageous to the point of not feeling the need to prove himself or to justify his speculating on the truth of what others took for granted.

In a sense Whitehead's effect was that of a shock, but of quite a different kind from that produced by Cohen, due largely to a difference in their personalities, manner, and aims. Cohen shocked through his questions and his actions, by his forcefulness and decisiveness. Whitehead shocked through his answers and his concepts, by his comprehensiveness and insight. The one tore away the error which obscured the face of truth, the other dimly revealed the truth he had somehow glimpsed. The one inquired, searched, criticized, proved, the other wondered, speculated, created, constructed.

One learned much, perhaps even more from conversations with Whitehead at his open house on Sunday evenings than one learned in his classes or from his books. Here Mrs. Whitehead and he spoke easily and freshly on whatever topic happened to come to the fore. They were at once charmingly witty and sage, at home in history and literature, politics and religion. The talk ranged on every dimension of existence, all participating—undergraduates, graduates, and colleagues—to the degree that they wished and could. There one grasped what it meant to be a civilized person in speech and in interest, to be appreciative of one's fellow being. At those times Whitehead lived out the philosophy he had technically explored. As he saw the world it was made up of many independent centers of activity, each forging, at every moment, a novel unity out of the inherited past and the relevant future, the focal point of both science and art.

By now I have forgotten most of the things I heard then and before. What remains behind, hardly touched by time, is the effect of the quality of mind and character, the impact of greatness, the feel of a Whitehead. With the years I have come to have less confidence in his philosophical system, though I think it to be the shrewdest presentation of the currently dominant Cartesian-Lockean view. But the spirit and the values he pointed to in thought and act remain unaltered, a still attractive goad and guide.

Teachers are constantly testing the young to see what items have clung to the memory; parents become worried when they hear the garbled propositions which their sons and daughters report as the latest truths glimpsed at college. Both, I think, worry too much; education is more a matter of learning the quality of a vision than it is a matter of learning that this or that item is true. Of course we must know details, master them, build on them; the point is that they remain insignificant and ineffective until caught within a vision which breaks through the confines in which we daily live.

At Harvard there was a room in Widener Library in which were to be found mounds of papers, the life work of an American philosopher, Charles Saunders Peirce. I had heard, through Morris R. Cohen, of Peirce as an unusually original mind who could not or would not fit into institutions and for whom institutions could find no place. In that out of the way room of the library, Charles Hartshorne could be discovered devotedly working on the Peirce manuscripts, trying to bring some order out of a chaos of hundreds upon hundreds of unpublished studies on a wide range of topics. He responded warmly to my offer to help, in part because my presence meant that he would occasionally see a face during the day. The existence of the six volume edition of Peirce's works which we published a few years later is a testimony to the feeling we and others had that a grave injustice had been done to Peirce during his lifetime and some time afterward.

Hartshorne and I were both deeply moved by Peirce. Here was

a man who, in the face of hardship and neglect, had devoted himself to a life of philosophizing. It is hard to conceive how, unheralded and ignored, suffering economic, social, and finally physical handicaps, Peirce could work hour after hour, day after day, year after year, on papers which he could not reasonably hope to see published. He said of himself that he had the persistence of a wasp in a bottle. The figure is singularly apt. Not only was he undeterred by what would have been insuperable obstacles for others, but he was always struggling to get outside the confines of his person, his environment, and his climate to the wider and clearer world beyond.

Peirce was to me then and still is a pathetic figure, a standing criticism of America's lack of self-confidence a number of decades ago. Peirce's tenacity and logical acumen place him in the forefront of modern thinkers. But such originality as his pays a high price to contemporaries. That price was nowhere higher than in nineteenth and early twentieth century America. The philosopher Peirce, the scientist Gibbs, the architect Sullivan, and the economist Veblen are but some of those whom America neglected a good portion of their days and cheated us who follow after of possibly greater fruits of their labors.

The life of learning is a lonesome one, but there is no need that it should be as barren as the world sometimes makes it be. A regrettable custom sanctifies the practice, that is all. We in America seem more frightened of our prophets than other nations are of theirs. Our greatest enemies we feel are those who utter new thoughts. We find it hard to withstand the incursion of novel major pronouncements—at least when their proponents are alive.

II

Persons primarily arouse the imagination; new places give it an opportunity to free itself from the fixed points about which it was accustomed to move. They make us aware that there are matters of importance which cannot be fitted within our habitual outlook. Unable to remain where we were, unable to stay where we are, unable to shift back and forth without becoming confused we, after visiting strange places, have no recourse but to adjust ourselves over the years to the unassimilated facts, tones, and values which we unconsciously stored away.

After getting my doctorate, my wife and I had the opportunity to study and travel abroad. I had by then not read much about the Continent nor had I studied or practiced any of the arts. I therefore came upon the pulsating, tolerant world of France and the art of Italy almost unprepared. I have still not entirely recovered from my sudden immersion in a world in which the past interpenetrates and often dominates the present to about the extent that the future intrudes and pervades our present action and thought. Such an encounter changes the center of our gravity. With time the images fade and little is left but the altered perspective which is no less pervasive and important because it is hardly noticeable even to one who suspects its presence.

Fortunately about the time I had begun to misremember, about the time my memory began to present my reading and conversations as the substance of the experience I had lived through and enjoyed abroad, I had the opportunity to endanger my equilibrium once again. Nothing in my life recently has equaled in importance my stay last spring [1951] at the Hebrew University in Jerusalem.

The University is in Jerusalem but not of it; it is not even integral to Israel. I do not mean that it is out of touch with the rest of the country or that it is uninterested in it or makes no contribution to it. The sacrifices of its faculty and its students, their contribution to the health, training, and scientific advance of Israel are too well known to make such a supposition even plausible. What I mean is that it has, as well, a European tone to it, and this not solely because so many of the faculty and students have a European background, or because it is European in its curriculum and rules, but because it has European knowledge and interest in the classics, a continental concern for ideas. Unlike our own, her scientists and philosophers are well acquainted with the history of thought, and are singularly able to follow and to enjoy creative thinking. Alert to subtleties, they were ready to discuss new turns of thought for whatever truth might thereby be gleaned. Taking into account its size, the Hebrew University is second to none, I think, in knowledge, interest, or sympathy for thinkers of all persuasions. I have never encountered audiences which were more perceptive, friendly, and critical than those provided by the students, the faculty, and the general public at the Hebrew University. Such places give imagination boundaries, dimensions, a meaning to be contrasted, a focal point and an inspiration.

III

Things, too, have a role to play in the arousal and sustaining of the imagination. The world contains people and places, but also a heterogeneity of objects, things of all sorts—big and little, active and passive, living and dead. Even if one did not have the good fortune to meet exciting people or to go to exciting places, he would in the course of a few minutes encounter enough to stir and charge the imagination. Everything is a center of mystery; inside the finite bounds of each there is an infinitude of content. Each is a bit of cosmic dust, a representative of the whole universe, complicated and complex, somehow holding to existence by a power apparently not all its own.

The world could conceivably have been otherwise. There is no self-contradiction in the idea that it contain quite different things than it does now. We can imagine each item, each occurrence changed radically or even destroyed. Indeed, it seems possible to think of everything whatsoever as not existent. Then why is there something rather than nothing at all? And if there could have been nothing, why is it that the things that are have this shape and not another?

All things are equally wondrous, differing though they do in importance and value. Any one of them can serve as an excuse for our turning away from the routine of prosaic living to become followers of an adventurous, inquiring spirit. Anything at all might serve a man as a clue to the nature of existence and of that secret which is at the heart of himself and others. It is possible, of course to be overcome with clues, to be overwhelmed by riches, to be overstimulated by what one encounters. It is foolish to allow our imaginations to be excited at any time or in any way that circumstances determine; equally foolish to refuse to allow the imagination never to be excited or when excited to deny it some free play. Both positivists and romantics do injury to their imaginations, the one by refusing it an opportunity to be quickened, the other by refusing it the opportunity to function as a controlled agency which discloses what lies beyond the obtrusive facts.

Here is a piece of stone. Like every other item in this universe it has a complex structure and some bearing on all others. It is intermeshed with all the rest to form a single contemporary whole; it is concerned, too, with possibilities which it realizes with more or less justice as it persists and acts through time. Each thing has its integrity, each has its independence, each has its value and its rights, but each, too, is subject to influences and constraints from without.

What this piece of stone will be it now can be, which is but to say it is now faced with possibilities which it realizes in some form or other as it carves out its career in time. But a possibility is a most evanescent thing; it is not palpable, not visible, hardly graspable even by the most abstract mind. I remember as a graduate student asking myself what a possibility is and whether a class of possibilities was itself a possibility or something else. The question drove me to study the writings of logicians who at that time spoke much about the nature of classes. Their theory of classes contained the incidental claim that the object of a proper name, Thomas or Prisiner 42, was an individual. I found this exceedingly strange. If the individual is the counterpart of a name, what is it that the predicate affirms, and of what does it affirm it? If "Thomas" is the name of an individual, "tall" or any other applicable predicate must be predicated of that individual. But if Thomas is tall already, the predication will be inane; if he is not tall, it will be foolish. If "Thomas is tall" is to state a significant truth, "tall" cannot be a predicate of what "Thomas" denotes. Together with "Thomas" it must instead serve to articulate the single unit, "tall-Thomas." It is this latter alone which is the individual, not a Thomas naked and cut off from his characteristics. The individual, in short, is the source of that aspect which we denote by a proper name and of that aspect we conceive and express by predicates. He is the ground, the substance, the locus of all the terms by means of which we speak of him and communicate regarding him. He is no momentary existence, perishing with the passing moment; he touches the future, the domain of possibility, and reaches outward into the environment to affect his contemporaries. The exploration of such considerations leads to the consideration of the nature of cosmic truths, each step of the way leading nowhere but to vain abstractions if not guided by the prospect of our being able to probe deeper into the wonder with which we began.

IV

Men tend to abandon habitual acts and thoughts most readily when they come across challenging minds and characters. There is no one of us I suppose who has not had the good fortune to meet men and women with conspicuous graces, contact with whom has made a signal difference to his life. And all of us perhaps have been at places which have helped us recognize new aspects to existence, possessed of unsuspected richness. Even those who have remained close to their birthplaces have been granted the occasional privilege of looking at themselves from a distance and thus have come to learn something of customs, ways and manners different from their own. Surrounding us is a miscellaneous, helter-skelter lot of things to which we can turn to learn what the world is like and what it allows us to be. Unless bemused by professional thinkers, there is, I think, no one but has found there an occasional foothold in the quicksands of existence, enabling him to make some advance in answering that why and how which is perpetually at the lips of every child. The more one contemplates any thing the more one sees how inadequate one's knowledge is, and how mistaken is the belief that it will yield its story if only one follow the lead of some science or philosopher.

There is no one way to the truth; there are many quite different ways, requiring us to move at different paces, each bringing results not readily obtainable along other paths. We learn what the world is in poetry and in physics, in philosophy and in history, but only if we allow ourselves to remark the mystery of things—which is but to say only if we allow our imaginations to be engaged, nourished, and guided by the world about, and then are willing to follow its lead beyond the boundaries of daily thought and need. The particular things we happen to know, the particular incidents which fired our imagination are a chance and minor selection from a multitude available every day and everywhere.

The spirit of God, the Bible begins, hovered over the deep. To say that man is made in God's image is but to say that he is one who does and ought to brood perpetually on what goes on beneath the surface of experience. It may be a person, it may be a place, and it can always be a thing which awakens, supports, and directs him in the hazardous but inevitable and desirable venture of knowing who, where, and why he is.

VI

THE ROAD TO UNDERSTANDING

BY

LYMAN BRYSON

When a man is asked to discuss the history of his own intellect, and has recovered from the flattering suggestion that he has one, he is bound to feel ambiguities in the assignment. After sober reflection, he feels sure that he will do best not to listen to what anyone else says on the same subject; an innocent ignorance will protect him from improper rivalries. And he had best trust the editor of the series to mean what he said. Moments of discovery are discoveries of the world outside and of one's own self, at the same time; this allows him a decent humility in self-exposure.

He sets out then to find in the attic corners of his memory, as well as in what is blazoned in the official versions, his own versions of his own life, what indications there are of the way in which a mind grows. He tries to locate turning points and realizes that such an assignment should be given only to a man of ripe years or to a philosopher who is wise before his term. I claim the first qualification. It takes about fifty years of adult experience, fifty years beyond adolescent dreams, to learn what one means when he talks about his own mind. And if we consider the "free" mind, which I mean to do, what does a mind free itself from, what fetters, what cobwebs, what inner twists? That is really my theme: what does a free mind have to learn how to shake off, and what burdens must be borne?

There are men and women who have to make their first struggle against being a disciple. But they have already gained much, before it becomes necessary to break away, from being disciple to

61

some kind of greatness and it could have been a misfortune for me that I never had that experience. I never found a man on whom I wanted to model my life. What is more, I never found a book which above all other books I could wish to have written. The disclaimer should not be misunderstood. It does not mean that I have not envied

"this man's art and that man's scope . . ."

often enough and to the point of weeping, too. But there was never the great advantage, or the incubus, of finding the master model in either life or works. I would have been a better man and ultimately free also, no doubt, if that had been my luck.

It is evident from this beginning that my subject is not that freedom of the mind which must be fought for against suppressions and interferences by governments or other institutions. These have existed all through my lifetime and I do not count on seeing the end of them. They are doing great damage in the world. But it has been my fortune not to run afoul of them in any way that mattered to my own program. They have caused me to suffer from pity and indignation and deep distrust, but not to hinder thinking. So, not only because of this providential advantage but also by reason of long study of myself and of my friends, I am convinced that internal chains on the free mind are far heavier and more subtly fastened than anything outside. We are bound by our fallacies and fears and mistakes.

We can begin the inventory with the fallacy of supposing that energy is a substitute for thought. It is natural to the young who have more energy than they can manage; for some persons it becomes a lifelong childish mistake. It is so old that it is embedded in a folk tale of Alexander the Great and one of the least heroic of his exploits is counted to him for honor. He cut the Gordian knot. My own stubborn attempts to expel this misunderstanding from the minds of students, in years of teaching, have been mostly wasted, so deep and so congenial to our animal enthusiasms is this silly picture of the great military mind.

You remember that there was a place (in Phrygia, wasn't it?) where the boy conqueror was wayfaring through. He was shown a cart in front of the city gate. On the front of the cart some Phrygian Boy Scout had tied a knot, very complicated and tight, and there was an inscription promising—I have never heard on whose authority the promise was made—the empire of India to him who untied it. Alexander, they say, looked at it, saw that it was a tough one, scowled, snatched a sword from a body guard, and cut it in two. Cheers! Everybody said, "That's the way a great man solves a problem!" Is that the way Alexander developed the phalanx his enemies could not break or won the battle of Issus?

He might have become the emperor of India if he had not drunk himself to death, but not by those methods. The fable does great damage to youngsters by confirming in them their natural instinct to evade problems with impatient violence. Great conquerors do not wield swords; they think. The Macedonian boy's head was a far more subtle and dangerous weapon when it took its time than a sword in his or any one's fist.

We are animals always, in spite of being also intellects and souls, and we have had millions of years of phyletic experience in our muscles and nerves to tell us that if we act quickly enough and resolutely enough and vigorously enough, it makes no difference how we act. Nothing can stand against us. But things do stand against us and our impatience batters itself uselessly on facts.

This fallacy, which we can call the worship of energy, has many forms. It was not the first shackle that I got rid of; it was the first shackle that I remember putting on and I can remember how I loved its heavy pressures on my young heart. Freedom from worship of energy was not reached until the years of college study at Ann Arbor, and the agency was providence or accident or just secular luck, not any search for relief. The lesson came, well disguised, in my acquaintance with a brilliant man, now dead, who never knew what he taught me. More of him later.•

There are two phases to this fallacy of effort in place of thought. The first is mere excited or dogged work, the animal stretch of the muscles. One of my neurologist friends, who is a scientist and hence knows how to put seemingly simple ideas into complex terms, says that this fault is a failure in telencephalization, a failure in the process of waiting before one acts. We have instinctive responses which do very well when we encounter a sabretoothed tiger in the morning jungle. They help to limber the muscles and alert the nerves. But when we meet a more modern kind of enemy, whose streamlining makes him more elusive and less merely physical, an enemy, for example, like a problem in personal relations, we cannot act very efficiently if we trust to bristling hair and good biceps. We need to back away from the problem. That seems to be in crude substance what Richard Brickner means by telencephalization and a burst of energy stands in the way of the deliberate thoughtfulness which makes it possible for us to meet intelligently a complex crisis.

The fallacy, however, is capable of catching us in more than one kind of net; the burst of energy can be transformed into a civilized industriousness which is equally enticing and untrustworthy. It was my luck to spend a year earning my own living between high school and college. A good many lessons in practical behavior which have been useful since were learned in that year and I began then a lifelong study of the ways of so-called practical men that has been a fascinating amusement. But I was pliant and imitative, and was on one side surrounded by earnest sober men who were getting slowly ahead to nowhere in particular, and on the other by young wastrels who kept up a reputation for genius by showing nothing but promise. Half my year was in an accounting office, half on the staff of a newspaper in a midwestern city. As between carousing genius and plodding mediocrity I could make no comfortable choice. The solution appeared to be that there must be such a thing as a plodding genius and that was what I would set out to be. Accordingly, I worked my head off, as I would have described it, omitting nothing in the way of long hours and breathlessness that would impress my betters. There is no record that they were impressed. By the time I went to Ann Arbor at the end of the year to continue my education, I had doubts. The college curriculum was a race that I expected to run, however, as a work horse.

As an aside, it should be said that nothing in this ought to be taken as lack of respect for hard work, whether by the intelligent or by the honest plodder. Indeed, one should go further and acknowledge that a lifetime of watching the careers of one's friends might well lead to the conclusion that they have differed among themselves more in power of work than in any other quality and that steady capacity for application to the main task is a major element in determining success. But that does not change the fact. Mere effort is a dangerous anodyne to telencephalization, to the more aloof but more intense thoughtfulness that unties the Gordian knots.

My discovery came from association with a brilliant, strange man, now dead, who came to Ann Arbor in my time. He was already in his middle thirties, much older than the rest of us because he had interrupted his college career to earn a living for his aged parents and was only now coming back to school as a junior classman. He had two children and an invalid wife. He had no money. But he had brains and an indomitable spirit and he understood some of the important facts of life. He was going to be an economist, he said, and I remember wondering by what inhuman expenditure of energy he could hope to get his graduate degree. We had some frank conversation but it was impossible to ask him the questions that pressed for answer. How could he expect to manage to live, to study, to undertake a difficult subject in which he had not yet got a start, become a scholar, and get a job?

His attitude taught me the lesson, by clear inference. These were only problems; one thought his way through them. Energy would not have solved them, although it was required; the very highest kind of industrious plodding would have been inadequate. Nobody but himself believed he could do it. But he did, and supplanted a few years later one of the professors of economics who had warned him not to try against so many handicaps. He went ahead to an academic career of high distinction and even made a fortune and lost it and made another before he died. A strange economist—to make money— and a strange man, but to me an impressive lesson in the power of courage and intellect. By stages, I saw that it was necessary to free one's self of the fallacy of mere energy if the mind was to be free. But that was only a beginning.

By the time I had left school, I had seen also that it was necessary to get free of the "book." I had then completed a course of which the first lesson, when I was a high school boy, was a true moment of discovery. It was a trivial incident but it seems impossible to equate the power of the lesson in these matters with the dignity of the occasion. Back in my high school days, we were reading Shakespeare with Kate McHugh, one of the great teachers in my life. In the midst of *Macbeth,* when I was dreaming of some combat far from Scotland, probably, I was startled to be called upon by Miss McHugh to identify a speech that had just been quoted. Was it by MacDuff?

My reply was "No," so confidently given that she should have been suspicious, but I was able to offer arguments as to MacDuff's character which bore me out. And then, abject slave that I was to the book, I was stricken in conscience. It was the merest bluff; there had been no clear memory of the page in the book where the speech was printed. This was a serious sin; I went to Miss McHugh to confess. When she learned that I had not really remembered what the book said, she asked how I had figured out my answer. The reply was, of course, that what I knew about MacDuff's character was sufficient indication that this speech would not fit him. "Bless you, my child," she said. "That is exactly what you should have done."

That was—I remember it well after fifty years—one of education's most valuable revelations. It was not necessary to remember precisely what was on every page of the book! Rather, one was expected to think what the book might have said, or should have said. With this new freedom it was possible for me to begin to peel off one of the worst kinds of enslavement, subjugation to the book, very common in our business and very dangerous to the free mind.

Having now begun to free my mind from mere energy and from the letter of the book, I found myself entangled with another obstacle and from that the way of freedom was harder to locate and tougher to travel. The mind also has to learn, if it is to be free, how to live with history. This does not mean the history in the books, or in men's memories, but the facts of one's own time and place.

The presentation of this problem came in the guise of an involvement, an unheroic involvement in the First World War. My job then was teaching in my own university and some family responsibilities had been acquired. Because of a wife and a baby, I was not drafted, but the whole country was like a pot aboil and it was not easy to stay in the classroom. A series of trials at getting into the center of things made it clear that I was a member of a "lost generation," the men and women who are too young at the beginning of a great war to be in charge of things and too old when the war is over to get a real chance. But there were accidents, in a series, which landed me after the war in Europe. There, for more than four years, I helped to pick up the pieces. The causes of such a chance for difficult, revealing experience may be accidents only in the necessarily imperfect view we have of the universe but there seems to be no reason why I should have had the chance to see so much of what war does to people and to learn it so well.

War displaces men and women. The evil peculiar to war is not death. Death comes to all men at some time or other. War displaces. Plans and institutions and habits no longer have any relation to actual living or any possibility of rational outcomes. Skills are wasted and accumulations lost and reputations are meaningless. People are no longer people when they are moved, helpless freight, from every possible connection with their past to places where they see no possible future. War is history in its most dire and inescapable form; it is the extreme lesson in the truth about the individual's place in the universe. This poses the deepest question of freedom. How can one be free of the temporal frame of his own brief chance at living?

My dose was a heavy one. The climax came in the winter of 1919–1920, when I went for the American Red Cross to the camp in Narva where the Yudenitch army of White Russians was dissolving. Yudenitch had got almost within sight of Petrograd but his 10,000 men were hopelessly outnumbered by Bolshevist armies and he retreated to the borderline between Russia and the little state newly freed from Russia, Esthonia. That little state, by the way, has long since been reabsorbed.

The nervous new government of Esthonia admitted the White army on condition that the soldiers surrender their arms. Thus they were saved from the Red defenders at their heels but an army without guns and, as it soon became, an army without officers, is a mob. The officers and medical staff disappeared and upwards of 8,000 men were soon down with typhus.

Hans Zinsser is possibly the only man who ever connected lice and history in explicit terms but the connection is an old one. The first day in Narva, where I was supposed to size up the situation and report back to American Red Cross headquarters in Paris, I was taken to an ancient stable of royal size where many hundreds of the typhus ridden soldiers were lying on straw in mangers and along the floors. My guide told me to keep a sharp lookout behind. I was, of course, indistinguishable in their eyes from any army officer and they would, I was told, be glad to chuck a louse at me as I went by. That was how they felt about Sam Browne belts.

History was there in death and squalor. Typhus is a filth disease and its victims require cleaning up even before they can be cared for. It was bitter cold. They were dying so fast that their frozen bodies were stacked against the outside of the barracks to wait like cordwood until the ground could be dug for graves. The little squad of American Red Cross officers, and the little squad of the British medical mission that was there with them, had to do something. They had to break that ring of dirt and dying. They began to bathe the men, to shave them, clean them up, clean their beds, and give them some idea of how to rest out the dangerous languors of their illness. Even that could not have helped much if it had all been done by the staff of sanitary angels. But heroism is, like cowardice, a contagious thing when it happens and before more than a few days had passed the Russian soldiers were beginning to help each other. The epidemic was stopped.

Out of this experience I learned a new lesson, one that still requires of me that I search out its meanings, but one thing was evident at the beginning. History cannot be escaped by the free mind. If you turn your back on the events of your time and place you are isolated, not free; freedom must always be in a world of real choices. And if your time and place demand work of any kind, no matter what, you are required to do your share of that, or it will haunt your freedom. You can do your share of the work but keep yourself detached from the violent and energetic partisanship which makes you a contributor to the next historical catastrophe. The lesson is difficult because to be active and detached, to keep true freedom of the mind in the midst of history, is a condition few can attain and only a few, not a much larger number, can see clearly enough to strive for.

It is reported of Goethe that he stood at the Battle of Jena and thought of the excellent material for the study of anatomy the dead and dying men around him could provide. This is the extreme of detachment and is repellent to our moral sense, so much so that we would like to believe that it is unjust to Goethe. The other extreme is to be so much involved in your own time that you compound old injustices and make new violence. It is given to some to contribute with simple heroism to the reconstruction of the tragically damaged, to give some comfort to the displaced. They are lucky examples. But no man can live a life so removed from human misery that he has no chances to hold out his hand in help to someone else.

One recent experience has made this difficult problem vivid in my own thinking. I went recently to hear the superb reading by Charles Boyer, Agnes Moorehead, Cedric Hardwicke, and Charles Laughton of the Bernard Shaw scene, "Don Juan in Hell." It is, you will remember, a little known part of the *Man and Superman* drama which is almost always left out of stage productions. These four read it straight, without costume or any kind of *diabolus ex machina*.

Charles Boyer as Don Juan, the reconstructed sensualist, is tired of Hell and wants to get away to Heaven where, he says—or rather, Shaw says—he can hope to think. Of the other three, Laughton as the devil and Miss Moorehead as one of Don Juan's secular victims, are content to stay where they are. Hardwicke, the old swordsman whom Don Juan had killed years before, and who to his surprise went to Heaven, is trying to get smuggled into Hell where he can relax.

You can remember the Shaw theme, developed here and elsewhere, that man was almost wholly detached from the procreative process, leaving that to Superman, the woman, so that he could develop a brain strong enough to comprehend nature itself, a part of nature understanding all of nature. And those who can take the truth can stand being in heaven.

It has sharpness and eloquence as it was read magnificently by these four. But what is it—truth? A satisfactory philosophy? The evidence and example of a free mind? It does not satisfy me.

I had to wonder if Shaw knew that love is a part of understanding. These are deep and difficult matters because if we are bold enough to say that it is not enough only to know, that contemplation is not enough as the whole purpose and accomplishment of human life, if we reject Goethe's detachment and Aristotle's contemplation because we feel that they are not enough, we are taking on great responsibilities. We cannot forget that the evil inherent in all action will infect us if we reject as evil an aware indifference. In all the ancient books, of the Indian East as well as in our own tradition, it is said that man has to act although he cannot hope ever to act in complete innocence. Is contemplation innocence? This is a question I have not been able to find an answer for. But a good dose of history with the sight and intimate smell of the degradation of humanity makes it difficult to believe that a free mind can escape being in some measure also a devoted mind. There are occasions in every man's life, it seems, when he has to stop trying to think and try to act, at whatever risk.

But the waves of history retreat and less serious matters take over our lives again and they have their lessons for us even after Narva and the typhus hospitals. After adventures and travels that yield nothing on our point, I came back to the United States, back home, and found a new impediment. Five years abroad, in Europe and the East, was enough to give me some perspective on home. Detachment had lasted long enough to free me, not from serious concerns but from many of the practical trivialities which clutter up ambitious lives. Then I discovered the menace of reputation. I had to begin the struggle against a reputation and found all my friends deep in its frustrations and defeats. Perhaps there is something in the excessive organization of American life, the bad side of our good habit of social action by free association, or it may be only our indecent habits of personal publicity, but something gives to the life of any American whose name is known a need to fight an unremitting rear-guard action against invitations.

My friends who are on the letterheads of the great world weep over wasted days and nights, foolish committee meetings, empty board sessions, noisy and pretentious conferences, and regret passionately their own silly speeches. But what can they do about it? Because associations are needed, to express in both opinion and action our common concerns, and also our independent rebellions, we are afraid to resist any busybody who has a cause or an idea. Among my friends are men and women who never can do anything as well as they are capable of doing it, who leave behind them not a record of excellence but a trail of half fulfilled promises, because they dare not say, "No," to a good cause, to a friend, or even to a prophet of the inevitable future. It has its humorous aspects but it is tragic, also, and it makes a lot of us mere sepulchres, buttered perhaps, which is less dignified than being whited.

What is the fault in these men and women who have lost the freedom of the mind by reason of an enslaving reputation? It is not lack of devotion to good ideas and good causes and I suppose it would be dangerous to suggest that there can be an excess in love of doing good. We are not offering a mere counsel of the golden mean to say that they are living lives less balanced and fruitful than they are capable of. The loss lies, I think, in the fact that they are working on the initiatives of others. There are subtle and difficult problems here, problems of power and effectiveness which we cannot go into and quite probably do not understand. But the crude phenomenon is so common to the experience of Americans that we are hardened to it and count it the normal price of what is called success. In fact, an able person who declines to be either a public figure or a committee slave is often called a public drone. Organizers say he lacks in public spirit, is uncooperative—which, indeed, he is. His reasons, however, may be sound. A free mind, given on chosen occasion to public service, should be more prized than a mere name and the fleeting personal appearance at a council table.

This is trivial in each separate event but it is the sort of commonplace cobweb that strangles the soul. Since it is slight, it can be overcome, strand at a time, by slight resistance. My insight into its real strength was again an accidental gift of time. A young promoter came to see me and ask that I make a speech on a program he was organizing. Very reluctantly—this was before I had learned my lesson—I said it was impossible for me to accept. There came then into the unguarded face of the emissary who had just finished telling me that I was absolutely indispensable, that the program would have to be given up if I was not available, that they had never even thought of anyone else, a look we can call the "next man on the list" look. It was written on his still solicitous but too candid face that he had already dismissed me from his mind and was only making a polite pause before exit. He was remembering on that little list he had in his pocket, where my name was already metaphorically crossed out—and it was probably sixth or seventh from the top, anyhow—the name of the next man who would get his sales talk. The door closes on his despair but he rings for the elevator with renewed resolution and residual hope.

This experience is reassuring, after you can get used to it. It is healthy to learn that you are not indispensable. One never learns the lesson for good and for ever, perhaps; I am still working at it. But in a fumbling, apprentice sort of way, I have learned to keep in my own imagination the strongest possible image of what I must do on my own initiative, for my own purposes, in order to resist the image of me which suits the purposes of others and which they are trying to shove into my attention.

The last obstacle to the free mind, in my experience, is one from which not even a saint can ever be free. In fact, I am not sure that saints are specially good at ridding themselves of it. This is the first, as well as the last infirmity of noble minds and minds less noble also, the desire for fame or recognition or credit or justice of any kind. Lord Morley, with a certain measured morality which he thought was complete, said you could do much good in the world if you did not mind who gets credit for it. The man with the free mind must go further: he must be content to do what he can in a world without caring whether or not anyone gets credit for it. Credit does not matter. Justice is not important as far as one's self is concerned. Justice to and for the other fellow, yes. You are responsible to the highest judgment for every little judgment you pass on others. You have to grant what rewards lie within your power to see that no one suffers or loses his right. But for yourself .many other things are more important and the fight for justice to me, needed sometimes for symbolic uses, can clutter my mind disastrously.

I have watched this in many of my friends. They are men of power and devotion and they belong to my party, so to speak. They fight for what I believe to be worth having and worth getting for others. It would be impossible to quarrel with their direction or their zeal. But they fret; they lie awake nights; they are discontent; they sometimes cannot see straight. They cannot do their best work because they are afraid it will not be known publicly who did what, or first did, or best did, what needed to be done, and some accolade of honor may be lost.

I would not pretend that I have arrived at this beatitude of simplicity and purity, nor that I can detect any great progress in my way toward it. But I have gone far enough to see that the love of justice to one's self, the defense of our own honor instead of care for the honor of others, among other things great or little, is a last bond upon freedom of the mind.

Sometimes one is tempted to think that it is true, the old saying that by the time a man knows how to live he no longer has any life left in him. But if you believe, as I do, that salvation comes from understanding, as the Greeks knew and as wise men in all later religions have learned from their ripest wisdom, then if you have lived long enough to gain some understanding, you have done all with your life that can be done in any length of time. It has been necessary to say that this freedom and understanding do not free us from action, action for which we are responsible to the highest judgment and which we take to further the good. But even this kind of action is not a substitute for trying to understand.

Men who think, and care about the effort to think, are easily seduced by the arch deception of Shaw which we spoke of earlier. In the voice of Don Juan, the tired sensualist, he describes a heaven which is a place for those who have mastered reality, who—he seems to mean—are just thinkers, reduced to incandescent brains. In them, the great ganglion of electric flashes has absorbed the love as well as the fear and stupidity of mortality. That sounds like the heaven of the free mind. But one begins to doubt, after a moment of repentance. One has to nerve himself to quarrel with Aristotle and Spinoza, too, if need be, as well as with Bernard Shaw.

Spinoza was, as I need not tell you, one who lived with a free mind. Although his spirit is profoundly alien to my own, in spite of the love and reverence one feels for so great a purity and power, one realizes that he spoke of some of the principles of freedom more deeply and better than anyone else. And he lived his freedom.

But he did not live long enough. That may have been an injustice to him and we can wish he could have lived longer to understand more. But he did not live long enough to have a loving grasp of life as well as an intellectual grasp, a grasp of what life means in tragedy and joy as well as in freedom. We have, I think, a quarrel with those who retreat into noble contemplation as a complete life, instead of wanting freedom for contemplation as part of life and perhaps its climax in wise old age. We cannot retreat from history, that is, from our own time and its problems, and, on the other hand, we have a right to the playfulness and caprice of freedom also, the artistry of thought which is the highest of the arts, what old Socrates had, although Plato the Puritan was tempted to take it away from him. We have a right to the tears and laughter of the mind as well as a responsibility for its highest and its most practical uses. Freedom, as the Puritan Plato also said, is for use.

And when we grasp all these things, our minds are free perhaps and if the juice of youth and human passions have not gone entirely out of us, we can live our few remaining years in that understanding.

VII

THE SUM OF IT ALL

BY

JOSEPH M. PROSKAUER

I regret that I have no manuscript for the classic address to which you are about to listen. I am rather busy, as Chairman of the New York State Crime Commission, and that leads me into fields very, very far from spiritual upliftment and moral integrity, and if at times I lapse into the lingo of the criminal investigator, you will forgive me.

But, I am going to try to make the few words that I shall say to you really a spiritual autobiography. This is the story of how my soul developed. This is my story of how I have come to believe that man's inhumanity to man which has made the countless millions mourn, is the most destructive force on earth, and why I believe that the struggle against that inhumanity, and for equal rights the world over, in America and everywhere else in the world, is really the struggle for the preservation of the Judaic-Christian civilization.

I was born in a little Southern city, Mobile. I was raised as a liberal Jew, not a conservative. I had a Negro mammy who, in all reverence, God rest her soul, was to me, I can say, a second mother. But I was born and reared with the prejudices and the antipathies that were innate in the culture and in the history of the South.

I came to New York. I was married to the lady who sits by my side, and in due time we had a daughter who reached school age. One day, I was taking this child to school, when we were joined by a little colored girl who was her classmate, and I found myself, this Alabama boy, who still retained some of his Alabama background, walking down Central Park West with my daughter clasping one hand, and this lovely little colored classmate clasping the other hand, I was talking to this little colored child. I found she was charming.

It suddenly flashed across my mind (this makes it one of those moments of spiritual discovery), "What are all these inhibitions, senses of prohibition that you have been harboring all your life?" That little incident was really the kind of eye-opening experience to me that began to make me think, and to feel—to think of the injustices, and to feel the injustices, that I knew had been heaped upon millions of my fellow human beings.

And, in the march of time, it fell to my lot to be the President of the American Jewish Committee, and there it was part of my duty, specifically, to fight anti-Semitism, a virulent form of bigotry, I developed more and more a passionate desire, which I have today, even in my declining years, to see this world a place free of bigotry.

It had been given to me, as a friend of Al Smith, to go about this country with him, in the 1928 campaign, and I saw there such exhibitions of anti-Catholic bigotry, that I acquired a sense of shame for my country, that in America, in a civilization proclaiming the high-sounding doctrines of equality, of Jefferson's Declaration of Independence, such things could be, in the land of the free.

So, I was developing a personality that approached this problem with passion. There came a time when the United Nations Conference loomed up in the future. And I determined to do what I could, at least, to implant into the law of the world, a sanction against bigotry and intolerance, wherever it reared its ugly head. I hope you will not find it tedious, but I would like to tell you some of the steps in the process.

There was in existence at that time, a Commission on the Organization of the Peace, of which Professor James T. Shotwell was the head, and we worked closely with them in their endeavor to shape a peace that would forever make impossible a recurrence of Hitlerian savagery.

And out of that cooperation, I, with some associates, drafted a declaration. I shall read a part of it to you:

With the inevitable end of Hitler, the struggle begins, not of tanks and planes, but of heart and soul and brain, to forge a world in which humanity may live in peace. This new world must be based on the recognition that the individual human being is the cornerstone of our culture and our civilization.

That all that we cherish must rest on the dignity of the person, of his sacred right to live and develop under God, in whose image he was created.

(And it continued to make this declaration:) That an International Bill of Human Rights must be promulgated, to guarantee for every man, woman, and child of every race and every creed and every country, the fundamental rights of human liberty and the pursuit of happiness. (A generalization, if you please, but a weighty one.)

Second, that no plea of sovereignty shall ever again be allowed to permit any nation to deprive those within its borders of these fundamental rights, on the claim that these are matters of internal concern.

And, if you think that is a generality, just remember what is going on in South Africa, under the plea that no United Nations, and no religion can interfere with the foul purpose of the political leaders of that stricken country, to damn its Negro, and its Indian population to mental and moral and spiritual and material servitude.

Three (and with this I shall end the quote, leaving the rest), Hitlerism has demonstrated that bigotry and persecution by a barbarous nation throws upon the peaceloving nations, the burden of relief from distress. Therefore, it is a matter of international concern to stamp out infractions of basic human rights.

And just as sure as there is a God in Heaven, the time will come when the world will have to pay the penalty of what is going on in South Africa today, unless the force of the United Nations can stop it.

With that preface, we went to San Francisco, where I had a quasi-official status as one of some sixty-odd consultants to the American delegation—I do not think many people know what that Board of Consultants was, and it was an interesting experiment. There was one representative from each of a large number of national institutions and societies. For example, the American Federation of Labor, and the CIO each had a representative. The Catholic Welfare Organization had a representative. The Protestant Council of Churches had one. The National Education Association had two representatives. The Jews had two, of whom I was one.

And we functioned. We used to meet every morning, and we were, in turn, met by a representative of the American Delegation, usually a member of it, and it was a two-way street. The State Department wanted to get to us information as to what was going on, and, in turn, wanted to get from us the impact of the great body of public opinion we represented on the course the Department was following.

And while that was going on, we began to hear rumbles about the fate of the human rights provisions of the Charter. For example, on April 26th, a newspaper dispatch said: "Many obstacles rise in the way of adoption," and one of the obstacles they listed, curiously enough, was that "the Soviet delegation is suspicious of any proposal which might eventually lead to interference with internal Soviet affairs." That was prophetic.

Another obstacle cited was the British opposition, for Irredentists in India, and other controlled British territories, might be able, under the International Bill of Rights, to cause serious embarrassment for Great Britain. Everybody seemed to have an interest in perpetuating some form of human servitude.

And the final comment was—the American delegation, though in principle behind an International Bill of Rights, may be split on adoption of such a Bill, in view of the fact that there is a marked division in the ranks of the delegation, as well as in the State Department.

We continued to agitate, and we had high hopes, and there came May 2nd—I will never forget the day—it was the last on which, under the rules, amendments could be offered by any of the great powers, to the Dumbarton Oaks proposals.

And that morning, Miss Virginia Gildersleeve, who was a member of our delegation, came before the Board of Consultants and told us that they had thrown up the sponge, that there would be no Human Rights proposals in the United Nations Charter. We swung into action. Clark M. Eichelberger for one, Professor Shotwell for another. I cannot remember the name of the Catholic priest who worked with me there, but he was a tower of strength, and so was Dr. O. Frederick Nolde, of the Lutheran Church, and we drafted a round robin.

We were to meet with the Secretary of State at four o'clock that afternoon. We circulated that round robin as far as we could. By four o'clock, it had been signed by more than half of the Consultants, and no one had refused to sign it.

That round robin, so far as I know, has never been published, except in my little autobiography. It was addressed to the Secretary of State. It specifically asked amendments to Chapter 1 of the Dumbarton Oaks proposals, by adding a new purpose, and that purpose was, "to promote respect for human rights and fundamental freedoms." It specifically asked the addition of a new principle—that is the way the Dumbarton Oaks proposals were divided—purposes, principles—and that new principle was this: "All members of the organization, accepting as a matter of international concern the obligation to defend life, liberty, independence, and religious freedom, and to preserve human rights and justice in their own land, shall progressively secure for their inhabitants, without discrimination, such fundamental rights as freedom of religion, speech, assembly, and communication, and to a fair trial under just laws."

We proposed to add to another section that described the work that the United Nations Organization was to do, in economic and social fields, that "of defending and safeguarding human rights and fundamental freedoms."

And, we specifically proposed the creation of a Commission on Human Rights. We urged, in that round robin, that the dignity and inviolability of the individual must be the cornerstone of civilization. I am quoting headlines on that. "Two, that the conscience of the world demands an end to persecution." "Three, that it is a matter of international concern to stamp out infractions of basic human rights."

And, lastly, quoting from Manley Hudson of the Permanent Court of International Justice, that each state has a legal duty—a legal duty!—"to treat its own population in a way that will not violate the dictates of humanity and justice, or shock the conscience of mankind."

And now I come to the climax of a Moment of Discovery. That round robin was read to the Secretary of State and his associates by my colleague, Dr. Nolde, and it fell to my lot to speak for it. I did. The incident has been described by Professor Shotwell. What he says is this: "As a historian, with all the careful reserves that a historian is bound to think of, I pay tribute. It was a magnificent victory for freedom and human rights." (If I may be personal for a moment, just as Jefferson selected his own tombstone inscription, I would like that inscription on my tombstone.)

I closed my appeal to Mr. Stettinius almost in these words: "Mr. Secretary, I am bound to you by close ties of personal affection and official loyalty. But I have this to say to you: 'You make a fight for human rights, and win, and bands will play, and flags will fly. You make a fight for it and lose, and we will still back you. You throw up the sponge without a fight, and there is not a man or woman within the sound of my voice, representing all these national organizations, that will not go out and fight you, sir, to the death.'" And you could hear a pin drop. I added, to my colleagues: "I have ventured to speak for all of you. I may have exceeded my authority. If there is anybody who differs with me, I hope he will speak up."

And I will never forget the way my heart went down into my shoes when Philip Murray of the CIO got up. "Mr. Secretary," he said in his genial Scotch burr, "I didn't sign that round robin." And then I was ready to faint. "But," he said, "the only reason I didn't sign it was, they didn't get it to me. Now, he said something about assuming authority. I am assuming authority to speak for my friend, Bill Green of the A. F. of L. over there, when I tell you that labor won't stand for your throwing up the sponge. You go out and make a fight for these human rights."

The Secretary jumped up and said, "I never dreamed it was like this. I am going up and call the delegation together." He did it. The delegation saw the light, and the Human Rights Provisions are in the Charter of the United Nations.

Now, so what? We have a Commission on Human Rights. They have drawn a Declaration of Human Rights. And, as always, they have spent endless time fussing around as to whether it is to include economic rights, and what definitions are to be included. I had not much interest in all those debates about words. The thing to do was get through a declaration on fundamentals.

Now they are engaged in creating the second document, a much more difficult one to create, a Covenant of Human Rights. That is the one that will have teeth in it. It has not been drawn yet, to anybody's satisfaction.

Do not delude yourselves into believing that the fight is won. When you see the Senate of the United States still pussyfooting about ratifying the United Nations treaty against genocide, you know that supernationalism is still rearing its ugly head in what should be a fair and decent world. The fight is not won. And there are ominous catastrophes on the scene. Nobody can be elated when he thinks of the town of Cicero. Of Miami. Of South Africa. And of other places.

And yet, I have that optimism which should always characterize old age. This has been an age-old fight. It will be an age-old fight. But now it is a fight in the open, and that is a great gain. We have got the snake out of the brush. And if Miami and Cicero be vile, as they are, the open and effective denunciation of them is to me as heartening as the barbarity itself was disheartening. And everywhere I see evidence, as I see here today, of men and women of every color, and every faith, rallying to the battle cry: "Down with bigotry, and down with inhumanity."

And I like to recall something that I said on another occasion, at Christ Church: What is the sum of it all for us Americans? I find it in the Christian Scriptures, quoting, let me add quickly, from the Hebrew Scriptures. It is where the man at law goes to Jesus and asks, "What shall I do to be saved?" And Jesus answers, "Thou shalt love the Lord thy God with all thy heart, with all thy soul, and with all thy might. And thou shalt love thy neighbor as thyself."

That, my friends, is the battle cry for all right-thinking and God-fearing men and women in the hard years that lie ahead.

VIII

THERE REALLY IS A GOD

BY

HARRY EMERSON FOSDICK

Biography and autobiography habitually reveal the importance of crucial moments of illumination and decision. That day John Keats picked up a copy of Spenser's poems is typical. The event was a catalyst, precipitating in Keats the imperative vocation to be a poet. Biographies commonly hinge on such decisive moments. Life stories are not smooth flowing streams, but turn unexpected bends for unforeseen reasons.

A fascinating book could be written on this aspect of life, as revealed in the biographies of well known men and women. On one side the tight squeaks, the narrow escapes, the thin ice that almost gave way, as when young William James, for example, decided to commit suicide, but didn't—how many hairbreadth skirtings of disaster biography reveals! And, on the other side, the casual chances that opened amazing doors of opportunity, the decisive moments of sudden illumination, the endlessly diverse illustrations of the fact that

> There is a tide in the affairs of men
> Which, taken at the flood, leads on to fortune—

most life stories have been profoundly determined by such crucial experiences. So Gibbon, puttering about the ruins of Rome on a holiday, suddenly was seized with the idea that he might write a history of the Roman Empire.

One feels very humble, however, about applying this fact to one's own life. Trotsky had gone only a few pages in his autobiography

before he exclaimed: "No man has ever yet succeeded in writing
his autobiography without talking about himself." That is the embarrassing trouble in any autobiography. Nevertheless, like any other
man, I can recall decisive experiences, and I shall dwell now on one
of the turning points in the development of my philosophy of life.
Religion had always been to me a matter of profound concern. When
I entered college I was deeply religious, untroubled by any doubts;
but by the end of my freshman year, I had completely blown my top.
I doubted everything. When I started for college as a sophomore,
I was in so rebellious a mood that a team of wild horses could
hardly have dragged me inside a church. I saw science and religion
in direct collision. I could not believe in God. At the beginning of
my junior year I told my mother that I was going to clear God
out of the universe, and start all over to see what I could find.
During that junior year, however, my deepseated concern about
religion got the upper hand again, and—while I had no idea what I
believed or could even believe—by the year's end I was making up
my mind at least to teach in the realm of religion—not preach!
What did I have to preach?—but to teach something in that domain,
perhaps comparative religion.

Then in my senior year I took a course in philosophy. Six of us
were in that class. One of them became a world famous biologist
at the Rockefeller Institute; another became a leading entomologist
at Cornell; another a leading figure in New York State's Department of Education; another held a similar position in Pennsylvania;
another became a leading New York City lawyer. We were a thought-
ful, serious group. Our professor did not try to indoctrinate us,
but he did face us in that course with the basic issues of philosophy.
One day we came out of the class room, a very sober group and,
standing on the steps of Alumni Hall, the boy who afterward became
one of the world's leading biologists exclaimed: "Fellows, there really
is a God!" I wonder if he remembers that. I never have forgotten it.
It was for me a crisis, a luminous moment of insight and affirmation.
I never have been able to escape it: "There really is a God." Of
course, I did not know it at the time, but my whole life's meaning
was determined then.

As always is the case with such luminous moments, many preparatory factors were precedent. Such crucial experiences gain their
power because suddenly they bring into clear focus what before had
been indeterminate and vague. And because my experience is rather
typical of many in my generation, I venture to speak of it to you
younger men, as revealing the kind of experience many of us old-
sters went through.

One precedent factor which made that luminous moment in
the classroom possible was, of course, my early training in a Christian home—an honest-to-goodness Christian home. We naturally
start in childhood with second-hand religion—religion by contagion,
unconsciously caught, if we are fortunate, from the infectious faith
and life of others whom we love and trust. Rufus M. Jones, the
Quaker leader, tells us that once, when he was a small boy, he ran
away from his proper job at weeding a turnip patch to spend the
day swimming and fishing, and, returning home at night, he knew
that he was headed for punishment. He got it, but in an utterly unexpected way. His mother led him to his room, put him in a chair,
and then kneeled down and prayed: "O God, take this boy of mine
and make him the boy and man he is divinely designed to be." Then
she kissed him, and went out, leaving him, as he put it, "in the
silence with God." As Rufus Jones afterwards exclaimed in recalling
the incident: "That was an epoch!"

I was reared in a home like that, and can recall just such epochal
experiences. They go deep with a sensitive boy. It takes some doing
to escape their persistent effect. A boy does not have to wait for
maturity in years before he experiences what Browning called,

> . . . moments, sure tho' seldom, . . .
> When the spirit's true endowments
> Stand out plainly from its false ones.

Undoubtedly, in that classroom's revelation years afterward, this
profound dealing with a supersensible Reality, of whose presence
my boyhood had been made so persuasively aware, was a major
factor.

Another antecedent factor, even more obviously operative, was my clearing away of a lot of religious rubbish which I had been taught in the churches. The worst enemy of religion is religion—its clutter of irrelevant, nonsensical, superstitious accretions, that insult intelligence and make faith seem ignorant credulity. Sometime since I discovered in an old book that I still possess, which was read to me as a boy, passage after passage like this about naughty children: "God will bind them in chains and put them in a lake of fire. There they will gnash their teeth and weep and wail forever . . . They shall not have one drop of water to cool their burning tongues." In my boyhood, when migrant evangelists came to town and heated it up for a revival, this hell opened its yawning mouth to receive us, and among the major sins, certain to land us there, were dancing, card-playing and theater going.

I was a sensitive boy—as I see it now, morbidly conscientious—and the effect of all this upon me was deplorable. I vividly recall weeping at night for fear of going to hell, with my baffled mother trying to comfort me. Once, when I was nine years old, my father found me so pale that he thought me ill. The fact was that I was in agony for fear I had committed the unpardonable sin, and, reading that day in the Book of Revelation, I was sick with terror.

Then later came intellectual difficulties—the incredibility of an inerrant Bible, the conflict of science with current obscurantism in the churches, the absurd denial of evolution, and all the rest. I could not stomach the nonsense. If this was religion, I was done with it. So, I made a pretty thorough job of being done with it, and, long before that classroom experience, I had emptied the baby out with the bath. I was through with all this incredible farrago of religion. But, then, in that class on philosophy, we faced the fact—a formidable fact—that we still had the universe on our hands. What about it? A mere chance collection of physical particles going it blind? And, quite unencumbered by theology or ecclesiasticism of any kind, I began to see what theism really means. Remember Matthew Arnold's lines:

> A bolt is shot back somewhere in our breast
> And a lost pulse of feeling stirs again. . . .

And then he thinks he knows
The hills where his life rose
And the sea where it goes.

Another antecedent factor, which lay behind that hour in the classroom was certain indubitable experiences of spiritual reality, which I could not deny. Long years afterward I ran upon a sentence of Canon Streeter, of Queens College, Oxford: "I have had experiences which materialism cannot explain." That sentence sums up, as I see it now, the basic reason why I regained my religious faiths. I had cast off all authority in religion; I believed nothing just because the Bible or the church affirmed it; I was on my own, fiercely independent in asserting that unless I saw for myself I would not give my faith to anything. But there were some experiences I *had* had for myself—factual, spiritual experiences that, the more I pondered them, the more I was convinced materialism could not explain. Wordsworth's familiar lines express my meaning:

. . . I made no vows, but vows
Were then made for me;
. . . that I should be, else sinning greatly,
A dedicated Spirit.

I had had such hours. You all have had them. Materialism cannot explain them. To say, as materialism must logically say, that they are caused only by physical particles going it blind along paths of least resistance in the brain, makes no sense. Conjure up all that materialism can conceivably explain, and there is still a *plus*—a momentous plus—experiential facts of the spiritual life. Even then, in my atheism, if I had run upon the statement of Boutroux, the French philosopher, about "the Beyond that is within, with which we come in contact on the inner side of our nature," I would have known what he meant. There is a "Beyond that is within." There is, as Tennyson put it,

That true world, within the world we see,
Whereof our world is but the bounding shore.

So I was prepared to come back to religious faith by the Quaker route. Even when I could not believe in God, I could not stop believing in the "inner light." We do have hours, as Sidney Lanier says, when

> . . . belief overmasters doubt, and I know that I know,
> And my spirit is grown to a lordly great compass within.

We do face conscience—the majestic sense of moral obligation— "Something inside a man that he cannot do what he wants to with." We do experience sin, guilty remorse, and forgiveness. And moral victory, too, snatched from the jaws of defeat by a Power greater than our own, is as real an event as sunrise. We do confront man's tragic history, where scientific brilliance brings him no peace if, gaining the whole world, he loses his soul. And we do confront godlike personality, disturbed, provoked, challenged, fascinated by it, and, if we will, ushered by it into a new life.

Such experiential facts are no more illusory or merely subjective than other objects of our thinking. We do not make them up. They are really here—pursuing us like "The Hound of Heaven" in Francis Thompson's poem. A wise theology clarifies them, reassures our faith in them, deepens our understanding of them, but, as for me, it is the experience itself in which I find my certainty, while my theological interpretations I must, in all humility, hold with tentative confidence.

These three factors, at least—boyhood in a really Christian home, an intellectual revolt that had discarded the obscurantism of the churches, and inward experiences which materialism cannot explain—lay behind that hour of clarification and illumination in the classroom. But that hour brought them into focus: "There really is a God." To be sure, that was only the beginning of a long, unending search. What kind of God? How to think about him? Where to find Him? How to explain life's cruel evil that seems to deny Him? But nonetheless, it was a notable hour.

I do not wish to exaggerate its clarity. It was no lightning flash. I hope that in this course some one may speak whose whole life was miraculously changed of a sudden—like Paul's on the Damascus Road. That can happen. Browning's description of such an experience is classic:

I stood at Naples once, a night so dark
I could have scarce conjectured there was earth
Anywhere, sky or sea or world at all:
But the night's black was burst through by a blaze—
Thunder struck blow on blow, earth groaned and bore,
Through her whole length of mountain visible:
There lay the city thick and plain with spires,
And like a ghost disshrouded, white the sea.
So may the truth be flashed out by one blow.

My experience was not dramatic like that. But it was a memorable hour. I still stand in the light of that hour's affirmation: "There really is a God."

I venture to add a few remarks about the outcome of such an approach to religious faith as my life story led me to. One of the crucial factors underlying all our theological controversies concerns the relationship between religious experience and religious doctrine. Some proceed as though the experience can come only after the doctrine has been accepted; others proceed as though the doctrine must be the intellectual explanation of the preceding experience. One party thinks that religion, while certainly involving spiritual experience, is fundamentally an objective truth, revealed to man, not discovered by him, stateable in dogmas not to be questioned but accepted and believed. The other party thinks of religion as rooted primarily in experiences of the soul, indubitable confrontations of man with spiritual reality which he must wrestle with in his philosophy, express in his ethics, and formulate as a proclamation of faith in his theology. To one party, doctrinal truth is central and permanent, while experience is subjective, variable, and not at all the underlying continuum and reliable criterion of faith. To the other, the soul's experience with spiritual reality is the fundamental fact, the datum which must be explained, and this experience grows as the soul grows, interpretation and experience interacting; it sloughs off outworn intellectual formulations and finds increased clarity and development in accepting new ones, so that doctrine changes while the basic experiences abide and deepen. Between these two ways of thinking there are many shadings, overlappings, compromises, but the difference is basic.

From the first point of view comes orthodoxy, whether fundamentalist or Barthian; from the second come all the varied forms of liberalism.

That second attitude in my generation kept many within the Christian fold, even when current theologies insulted their intelligence. Out of a critical and to them momentous struggle, on which the whole meaning of life depended, they bear witness that not so much theology as experience is the abiding continuum underlying vital faith. So Jeremy Taylor put it long ago: "Men cast out every line, and turned every stone and tried every argument: and sometimes proved it well and when they did not, yet they believed strongly; and they were sure of the thing when they were not sure of the argument."

In this approach to religion's reality, I was confirmed by the teacher who, more than any other, influenced my young manhood—William Newton Clarke. He was a great spirit, profoundly and vitally Christian, to whom the creative experiences of personal religion were intimately real. His major effect on me was to outflank my intellectual difficulties. He always went back, behind the forms of doctrine, to the basic and abiding experiences of which they were the transient and often dispensable expressions. He made essential religion live for me again, real and vital, and let the mental formulations trail along afterward as a matter to be taken up at the mind's leisure. To use his own comparisons, he was sure that the stars were there, though we might have to change our astronomies, and that the flowers were real, though botany might alter its explanations.

As for my own thinking, I have never been either a theological reactionary or a theological radical. I could not be a theological reactionary because, so it seemed to me, the fact that while stars abide astronomies change is a true analogy, so far as it goes, of every realm of human life and thought, religion not least of all. No existent theology can be a final formulation of spiritual truth. Concerning every human experience theories of explanation and interpretation are essential, but, however confidently they may be held, their probable insufficiency must be assumed and their displacement by more adequate categories positively hoped for. Cosmic theories and theologies are meant to change. Static orthodoxies, therefore, are a menace to the religious cause. If the day ever comes when men care so little for the basic religious experiences and revelations of truth that they cease trying to rethink them in more adequate terms, see them in the light of freshly acquired knowledge, and interpret them anew for new days, then religion will be finished.

Unable to be a theological reactionary, I could not be a theological radical either. The radicals I have known always seemed to me to have decided that something serious had happened to the stars because an old astronomy had gone. My own reaction has been the opposite; the old astronomy was wrong about something real, and to get at that reality afresh, to see it again more clearly and more truly was the only solution that in the end counted for anything. I have been commonly accused of taking theology too lightly because I have been eager for new ways of seeing and putting Christian truth. Upon the contrary, I take theology so seriously that whenever, in the Christian tradition, I see doctrine persistently struggling over some central issue, displaced by new doctrine but still tussling with the same old problem, I am sure that truth is really there, and that the combined transiency and persistence of doctrine in dealing with it is a testimony to its importance. So ideas of God change and ought to, but that does not mean that anything has happened to God; and theories of the atonement have followed one another in a long succession, but far from undermining the significance of vicarious sacrifice, that only bears witness to its inescapable momentousness. The radicals throw out the baby with the bath.

Such in brief has been my religious life story. To put the matter into a single sentence here is my position: Just as around our bodies there is a physical environment, from which we draw bodily life and strength, so around our spirits is a Spiritual Environment with Whom we can live in vital contact, and from Whom we can draw power, guidance, and peace.

IX

HOW TO LIVE CREATIVELY AS A JEW

BY

MORDECAI M. KAPLAN

I share with my colleagues in this symposium the reluctance to be vocally autobiographical. One indulges in such autobiography, as a rule, only on birthday anniversaries. To overcome that reluctance I have had to make use of a lesson once taught me in my late teens by a teacher whom my father had engaged for the purpose of dispelling my doubts concerning the Mosaic authorship of the Pentateuch. That teacher was an ardent follower of Hasidism as well as a philosopher. I once asked him how could Moses have written the verse in Numbers which reads: "And Moses was the humblest of all men on the face of the earth." His answer was that the saintliness of Moses enabled him to achieve such self-detachment as to be capable of speaking about himself as though he were somebody else. That answer did not satisfy me as to the question of Moses's authorship of the Pentateuch, but it taught me a lesson in the art of self-detachment. When a person has to speak or write about himself, he should do so as though he were speaking or writing about somebody else.

I

All my life as student and teacher I have been preoccupied with tradition, civilization, and religion in their relations to one another. Whatever moments of discovery or illumination have lit up my career I owe less to books and more to my having had to grapple with one of the toughest problems in social and religious adjustment, namely, how to live creatively as a Jew. If I venture to unfold to you the story of my inner struggles, it is because I believe that it may have something to say to those who are still wrestling with the tradition, civilization, or religion in which their lot is cast.

The problem of how to live creatively as a Jew has obsessed me since my thirteenth year when I entered The Jewish Theological Seminary of America as a student of the preparatory class. The only word in that formulation of the problem which was not present in my mind at that early age was "creatively." The very idea of living creatively emerged long after I attained maturity, but as I look back on my entire career I note that it was implicit as a desideratum in all my searching and striving.

I ascribe my obsession with the problem of how to live creatively as a Jew to the fact that the first years of my life I lived a full and satisfying life free from all competing or complicating interests that might have created difficulties or inner conflicts in attempting to live as a Jew in non-Jewish surroundings. I then lived in what was practically an all Jewish town in Lithuania not far from Vilna, which was the part of the world then known as the Russian Jewish pale. I heard and spoke only one vernacular, Yiddish. I knew of and attended only one kind of school, an all day Hebrew *heder*. I knew and studied only about one people, the Jews. I knew and studied only one literature, the Bible. I looked forward to only one kind of rest day, the Seventh Day, Sabbath, to only one set of holidays, those of the Jewish calendar. The only games I played besides hide and seek and shooting nuts were based on Bible stories such as those about Samson and the Philistines, David and Goliath, David and Jonathan. The only public mischief I indulged in was on the fast day of the Ninth of Ab, when I would join my playmates in throwing burrs on passersby.

The first occasion when being a Jew became a problem to me was, when as a child of seven, I migrated with my mother and sister to Paris, at the same time that my father, whose long rabbinic training had qualified him for a Jewish academic or rabbinic post, migrated to America. On the second Sabbath after our arrival I remember attending school, and being asked to write out some lesson. In order not to transgress the prohibition of the Sabbath, I told a fib. I said that my hand hurt me. The next Sabbath I stayed away from school. My predicament was resolved during the week following. My mother found a small apartment in the Jewish section of Paris. There children were free from school on Saturday and Sunday instead of Thursday and Sunday as in the schools of the rest of the city. The second occasion, when being a Jew became a problem was about a year later when my mother, my sister, and I were on board a French steamer bound for New York. We were in steerage. It was Friday night. Announcement had been made that there would be fireworks on deck in honor of Bastille Day. I was eager to join the crowd to see the fireworks. But my mother would not permit me to go before reciting my Sabbath Eve prayers. By the time I was through the fireworks were over and I was left brokenhearted.

When I was brought to this country at the age of eight, I lived on the lower East Side for nine years. That neighborhood was then predominantly Jewish. My studies were almost entirely in the field of Bible and Talmud until I was twelve years old. At twelve I entered public school, but continued my Jewish studies without interruption, because my parents had chosen the rabbinate as my calling. From that time, my life has been an endless quest for a *modus vivendi* between two worlds, two universes of discourse, two civilizations, the Western and the Jewish.

Due to the sheltered surroundings in which I have always lived, I have never come in direct contact with anti-semitism or anti-Jewishness. I have always lived among Jews and have never had to seek a livelihood among non-Jews. The awareness that vast numbers of Jews find it hard to be Jews because of illwill and discrimination has always come to me indirectly. That may account for my tendency to rate anti-semitism as a secondary and not as a primary Jewish problem. I have always been concerned more with what would enable the Jew to live creatively than with how he might avert the hostility of his neighbors. On the other hand, it is understandable why Jews who have only an indirect knowledge of Judaism should be preoccupied with combating anti-semitism as often for the purpose of being permitted to pass off as non-Jews as for the purpose of not being penalized for being born Jews. That preoccupation is euphemistically called "community relations," and in recent years has reached a scale of duplication and competition, which has made it necessary to call in the advice of Professor R. M. MacIver. As far as I know, it has been, culturally, quite sterile even in terms of human relations, although it will probably serve as useful material for further discoveries in phychoanalysis.

My environment and upbringing had thus conditioned me for dealing with the question of how to develop a type of society which would correspond not to a circle with a single center but to an ellipse with two foci. This is what I mean by living in two civilizations. How to live simultaneously in two civilizations is a question which should concern not only Jews but also Christians and Moslems. Why that is so, will, I hope, become clear as I proceed.

During my adolescent years, in the midst of my college and theological studies I came under the influence of the greatest modern Jewish exegete, Arnold B. Ehrlich. He opened my eyes to the Bible as a composite human document, the original meaning of which lies buried, for the most part, under the many layers of commentary. Ancient commentators generally read meanings into the texts rather than out of it. In addition, I became acquainted with the works of Higher Criticism, which destroyed for me not only the strictly traditional assumption that the Pentateuch was dictated by God to Moses, but even the more modern one that it was all the work of Moses. For a few years I struggled with that problem, upon a satisfactory solution to which depended my continuing in the rabbinate. Loss of belief in the Mosaic authorship of the Torah and in the historicity of the miracles recorded in it seemed to me then as ominous to the survival of Judaism as the destruction of the First and Second Temples of Jerusalem must have appeared to those who witnessed them. I went through my storm and stress period during the first decade of this century, when the Zionist movement, despite its seemingly quixotic character was beginning to make headway in this country. From the very start that movement had an ambivalent character. The Zionism promulgated by Theodore Herzl, as a movement to establish a Jewish state, was a reactive response to anti-semitism. As such it was a means of salvaging *the Jews* from impending doom by finding for them a haven of refuge. The Zionism promulgated by Ahad Haam was a *creative* response to the disintegration of *Judaism*. As such it spelled the rebirth of Judaism in the land of its origin.

As an American Jew, removed from the European scene, I was troubled much less by the menace of anti-semitism than by the disintegration of Judaism. I experienced that disintegration in my own person, when the Bible and the Talmud lost their authority for me. At that juncture in my life Ahad Haam came, as it were, to my rescue. His series of essays entitled, *At the Crossroads,* made me realize that Judaism did not depend upon the authoritative character of the Bible and the Talmud but upon the will of the Jews to live as a people. That was a most illuminating moment in my life. It opened up new vistas of thought and spirit. It revealed to me the existential reality of the Jewish people. I became poignantly aware of the Jewish people, in the same way as we become aware of our country when it is threatened by invasion. This poignant awareness then afforded me the spiritual anchorage I sorely needed.

I discovered that the essence of living as a Jew was the acceptance of belonging to, and self-involvement in, the life of a people animated by a common will-to-live. The potency of that common will-to-live of the Jewish people was such as to find expression in a common history, in a common tradition, and in a sense of common destiny. No matter how much I doubted the historicity of the miracles and the supernatural origin of the Torah, I could not doubt the existence of the Jewish people and its claim upon me to help it live creatively. It was at that point that the nature of my conditioning during the first seven years of my young life bore fruit. It helped to give body to the notion of the existential reality of the Jewish people, for it convinced me that the Jews had enough in their own unsupplemented way of life, all that was necessary for living a full and good life, all that we associate with the term, "civilization."

II

Our inner problem as Jews was, therefore, not how to maintain the infallibility of a tradition but how to save our people from dissolution. The problem was how to get its men and women and children to retain and maintain their sense of oneness. That sense of oneness had never been challenged before the advent of modern nationalism. For, as long as Jews were kept out of the general body politic, their very segregation reinforced their will-to-live as a people. But with the advent of the modern nation that no longer required church affiliation as a condition of citizenship, and with the incorporation of Jews into the general body politic, their status as a people has become increasingly ambiguous. That ambiguity has had a corroding effect on the will-to-live as a Jew, an effect that mere religious revival, whether orthodox or modernist, cannot counteract. It is impossible for Judaism to exist without Jews, and it is impossible for Jews to exist without an identifiable, status-possessing Jewish people. Jews today are actually like veterans of a disbanded army, mistaking their periodic parades for military service.

It was this interpretation of the crisis in our inner life as Jews that opened my eyes to the need of effecting a Copernican revolution in the very understanding of Judaism. More important than modernizing it was seeing it in its proper relation to the Jewish people. Instead of Judaism occupying the center of the constellation of Jewish values, with peoplehood revolving around it, I discovered that peoplehood always had held and should continue to hold the center, with Judaism revolving around it. I thus came to see Judaism as the creation of the Jewish people as well as its molder, in the same way as the character which a person achieves gives meaning and direction to his life. So viewed, Judaism cannot possibly be limited merely to what is generally spoken of as a religion. The land of Israel, for example, which the Jewish people has made into a house word of its own religion as well as of Christendom and Islam, or the Hebrew language into which it has breathed its own spirit, are as integral a part of Judaism, as its religious beliefs and practices. On the other hand, those religious beliefs and practices have been able to keep the Jewish people alive throughout the centuries that it has been a wanderer in many lands where it evolved vernaculars other than Hebrew. If the Jewish people is to recover its capacity for creative living, especially outside the land of Israel, its religious beliefs and practices will again have an indispensable role to play.

It is thus evident that, from the standpoint of creative Jewish survival, we are in need of two distinct though integrally related categories to operate with, one for the entire complex of land, language, laws, folkways, mores, institutions, and agencies through which Jews have been interacting individually and collectively and experiencing their sense of oneness as a people. That is the Jewish civilization. Judaism is as appropriate a term for that as Hellenism for Greek civilization and Americanism for American civilization. On the other hand, the particular aspect of the Jewish civilization which relates to the belief in God should be specifically designated as Jewish religion. A religion embodies universal truth in particular circumstances.

This meant to me more than an exercise in semantics. The logical distinction between Judaism and Jewish religion necessitated my exploring (in a spirit which Jewish scholarship has thus far not felt called upon to do) the psychology and sociology of religion in general. The early Reformers, a century ago in Germany, treating the survival of the Jewish people as merely incidental to the adjustment of Judaism to modern life, philosophized about Judaism as a religion and thought their job done, when they succeeded in proving to their own satisfaction that the God idea in Judaism was truer than the God idea in Christendom. I, however, was not interested in proving that superiority of the Jewish idea of God, for even if it were superior, that fact would no more motivate one to be a Jew than the superiority of Aristotelian philosophy to that of any other would lead one to become a Greek. From the very standpoint of the conservation and development of Jewish life I had to know how the belief in God arose and functioned in relation to the other elements in a civilization. I sought to learn from my readings in the human sciences what human needs religion satisfied, and which among those needs nothing but religion can satisfy. Once I could identify those, I would know how Jewish religion had to be reconstructed so as to motivate in the Jew his will to live as a Jew and to have his fellow-Jews reconstructed as a people.

III

As the outcome of my studies it dawned on me that all our misunderstandings of the place of religion in human life arise from the failure to distinguish between religion as a social phenomenon and religion as an individual experience. While one cannot exist without the other, to fail to distinguish them when we deal with religion, is to get ourselves caught in our own traces. The difference may perhaps be made clear by an analogy.

Take the case of language. One person by himself could not create a language. Its beginnings are unself-conscious. Its main function is to be a means of communication among people. As such, it is a social phenomenon. On the other hand, whatever each one of us says or writes, whether it be as part of conversation, as a letter or as a poem, is an individual expression, which would not have been possible without a preexistent language. Likewise religion, as a social phenomenon, makes societal continuance possible. It confers unity and continuity upon a people, church, or nation. Religion, as individual experience, is the awareness of some supersensible reality as impelling us to do our best and enabling us to bear the worst that befalls us. When, for example, someone who has been brought up in a religious home, at first rebels against all religion and then in a moment of illumination or self-discovery experiences a religious awakening, that awakening could never happen, if he had not been conditioned religiously in his early years. Out of nothing nothing comes. That early conditioning in the home is religion as a social phenomenon. That personal awakening is religion as personal experience. The recognition of the difference between those two functions of religion can help us, like Ariadne's thread, to find our way in the labyrinth of theological, scientific, and philosophic discussions of religion.

In religion as a social phenomenon, God is conceived as the guardian of group spirit in which the individual needs to have a share. That phase of religion develops rituals which call for public participation, and which foster a sense of unity with the society of which one is a part. The effect of their observance by the individual is assumed to be experienced by the entire group. Religion in this instance is synonymous with loyalty.

Moreover, it is in religion as a social phenomenon that God is conceived as the author of laws which make for satisfactory human relations. Those laws are both ethical and juridical. They are attended by sanctions, some to be experienced by human hands, and others by divine power. Religion of this type tends to stress the primacy of justice, responsibility, and love.

From the standpoint of religion as group expression the difference between one religion and another is like the difference between one civilization and another. It is a difference of otherness and not of unlikeness, an existential and not a conceptual difference. It is like the difference between one person and another, no matter how much alike they may be qualitatively, in appearance, character, fortune, or what not. Each religion occupies a distinct area of human experience.

This existential difference among religions is secured through their respective *sancta*. The *sancta* are the constellation of heroes, objects, places, texts, events, and occasions which figure as having to be reckoned with or as agencies through which the fulfilment of religious needs are attained. Each religion has its own constellation of such *sancta*. These give each religion its individuality and existential otherness.

Besides the recognized purpose which *sancta* serve for the adherents of the particular religion to which those *sancta* belong, they serve two other unintended but nevertheless highly important purposes. First, they make possible the sense of continuity in a religion, despite the changes it undergoes as it passes from one generation to the next and from one environment to another. The sameness of the heroes, texts, objects, etc., gives those who cherish them as *sancta* a feeling of identity with those who cherished them in the past, despite the different interpretation which they receive, or significance that comes to be attached to them. Secondly, they serve a purpose for which there was no occasion in the past. In modern times the increasing diversity in men's thinking would quickly tear a religion into fragments, if it were not for the identity of the *sancta* through which a religion functions. That it is which makes it possible for Jewish, Christian, and Moslem religions to retain their respective individualities, despite the fact that ideologically there may be more in common among progressive believers in all the three faiths than there is between them and the fundamentalists in their own faith.

This understanding of group religion points to the way in which Jews who have cast their lot with other nations can nevertheless manage to live creatively as Jews. As American Jews, for example, we have the opportunity to illustrate what it means to live in two civilizations with advantage to both. Maintaining Jewish life would then mean living Judaism as a civilization and not merely as a religion. That calls for the establishment of organic communities to replace the present chaotic aggregate of *ad hoc* organizations. Such organic communities would be part of the Jewish people which would be the true analogue of the visible church in Christian civilization.

Our integration as Jews into American life, on the other hand, should mean much more than sharing its political, economic, and cultural life. It should foster in American life the method by which all civilizations in history have achieved religious self-expression, namely, by signalizing its *sancta*. Not only military and political heroes but all outstanding creative personalities in the life of our country, all events, places, objects, and texts which have played an important role in its progress, should be interpreted in the spirit of religion as loyalty, responsibility, justice, and love. Our national holidays should be made into occasions when that spirit of religion would achieve public expression. A beginning in that direction has recently been made with the publication of the volume, *Faith of America,* in which an order of public worship is built around thirteen of our American holidays, including U.N. Day.

IV

From the standpoint of religion as personal experience, God has been conceived in ways corresponding to the prevailing conception of what constitutes perfection or salvation. Thus religion as personal experience has given rise to the following conceptions of God which answer the personal needs of the individual:

1) God as the Power that enables the individual to attain what he needs in terms of personal goods, such as health, security, and approval. To those to whom God means that, religion, on the lowest scale of cultural development takes the form of magic and theurgy. On a higher scale, it takes the form of religiosity, which consists in a meticulous observance of rites, in expectation of being rewarded with the fulfilment of those needs; and on the highest scale, it takes the form of piety, in which rites are carried out in a spirit of trust that somehow they will bring their earned reward in the here or in the hereafter.

2) God as the Power that satisfies man's need to feel at home in the world, the need to believe that his life has meaning and his values durability. Religion of this type gives rise to faith. In its various forms of prayer and worship the main aim is to strengthen morale.

3) God as the Power that enables man to transcend death. This conception of God ties in with the assumption that man cannot achieve fulfilment in this world, but only in heaven, or in some world beyond. Religion based upon this conception of God, though having much in common with all the preceding, is fundamentally otherworldly, whether or not it find expression in ascetic attitudes and practices.

The foregoing is a brief summary of the way religion functioned as personal experience in the past. If it is to continue to function as such in our own day, it has to satisfy some over-all need of human nature of which the three needs enumerated above might be regarded merely as special forms that reflect particular stages of cultural development. Such an over-all need is that for perfection, salvation or self-fulfilment. God would then come to mean the Power that makes for salvation.

The problem of personal religion nowadays, therefore, is not the metaphysical one of how to conceive God, but the psychological one of how to conceive salvation. What we need is that understanding of human nature which would help us recognize in reason, wisdom, and love, the manifestations of a Power which operates throughout the universe. That is the Power which impels every individual from the electron, through man, to the furthest constellation, to be itself and at the same time to seek to integrate itself into some larger entity. We encounter that Power in every cell of the body and in every thought of the mind. That is nothing less than the encounter with God.

If religion is to function as personal experience it will have to answer the need of the individual to find life worthwhile and to help him make the best use of it. That is a task which all religions have in common. It is only as social manifestations that they differ from one another. Their differences are existential rather than conceptual, in so far as they are embodied in distinct corporate entities known as churches or peoples. Each religious body has a life of its own, and a will of its own to enhance that life. That is their God-given inalienable right. Only by learning to live together in freedom and peace will they speed the day when the Fatherhood of God and the Brotherhood of Man will become a reality.

X

A PHILOSOPHER MEDITATES ON DISCOVERY

BY

RICHARD McKEON

Novelty and discovery are subjects which elude analysis and discourse, for novelty, in the degree that it is intelligible, is familiar, and processes of discovery, if they could be reduced to rule, would differ little from customary actions guided by precept or habit. The inspiration which led the artist to a new form is reduced to technique or banality when he tries to explain how the idea occurred to him in any way other than by another artistic or poetic creation as mysterious as the first. The discovery of new scientific principles is lost in the accounts of antecedent ideas and attendant circumstances which explain neither the occurrence nor the novelty of the discovery. New insights in religion, even when they do not appeal to the operation of supernatural powers, are not reducible to formulas within the voluntary control of human agencies. Mathematics is the only field in which heuristic principles can be stated in a precise, abstract form and can be given practical application in the solution of problems, and it is possible there only by use of knowledge of an underlying order. In general, the discussion of discovery and of the occurrence of new ideas and insights must take the form either of a psychological examination of what goes on in the mind (and the crucial moment of discovery must then be assigned to the subconscious), or of a sociological study of influences (and the novelty of the discovery must then be found in the peculiarity of one man's response to what is common), or of a formal statement of guiding principles (and the discovery must then be sought in the possibly vacuous region surrounded, and progressively delimited, by those principles). During periods in which logicians have been concerned with problems of discovery and proof rather than with language and modes of expression, controversies in logic have often turned on the paradoxes of discovery, as when Mill criticized Whewell's "logic of discovery" on the grounds that discovery cannot be reduced to rules, and Whewell criticized Mill's inductive logic on the grounds that it only verified what had been discovered and omitted the problems of greatest importance to the scientist and the logician.

Discovery in philosophy is involved in the same paradoxes as a discovery in art, natural science, mathematics, and religion. Yet the universal scope of philosophy, and the divergent forms which philosophic speculation takes under the influences of analogies borrowed from art, science, mathematics, politics, and religion makes the profession of a new philosophical discovery at once more presumptuous (since the field is so large and the ground so well explored) and more modest (since the discovery of the new is scarcely distinguishable from the rediscovery and restatement of the changeless). Philosophy is a form of personal expression, of social integration, of scientific formulation, and of insight into fundamental values. In each of its forms, the approach of any philosopher is novel and the statement of his philosophy is a discovery, yet it is determined by conditions and circumstances which include the statements of other philosophers, the habits and institutions of men, the knowledge of scientists, and the underlying values that assume different forms in great varieties of expression, institution, and knowledge. Any given discovery is a function at once of the psychological experiences of one man and of the patterns accessible to all men whose experiences evolve in the common setting. Viewed as a personal expression of values, philosophy is an activity in which all men engage: we are all, willy-nilly, philosophers, and our originality is part of our character and individuality. Viewed as a social adjustment to times and circumstances, philosophy expresses shared attitudes, common cultures, and accepted values: we are all philosophers in a sense which transcends personal and esthetic differences in so far as we are sensitive and sympathetic to the values of those with whom we are joined in association and community. Viewed as a form of knowledge, philosophy is a systematization or integration of experience, science, and values: any one who reflects on his situation and his actions, his origin, nature, and destiny, is a philosopher in a sense which transcends personal and social differences in so far as he seeks common principles governing the interrelations in his life and in his understanding of what he perceives and what he knows, what he undergoes and what he seeks. Philosophers who aspire to that name as their particular designation (if only in the catalogues of universities in which they carry on their speculations or in the names of learned societies which they join) differ from these more numerous philosophers primarily in the fact that they relate their philosophic activities in personal expression, in social communication, and in scientific formulation explicitly to the basic values which they seek to realize. The peculiar psychological processes by which the philosopher is led to novelty of form or content takes place, therefore, on a background of historical, cultural, and intellectual constants.

The claim of novelty and discovery is frequent and recurrent in the history of philosophy. In a sense, the same thing has always been discovered, if we are to believe the claims that have been made—and the claims that are being made—and yet the novelty is in each case genuine. This pattern of reiterative novelty was set at the very beginning of the history of philosophy in the West. Socrates, according to Aristotle, was the first to apply the scientific method, which had previously been used only in physics, to the affairs of men—or, as Cicero repeated the novelty of Socrates's achievement, he first brought philosophy down from the heavens and gave her habitation in the cities of men. Both of the persistent elements of philosophic novelty are present in these statements of discovery—the use of science and the concern with values. Aristotle professed to have continued the task where Socrates left off, and Cicero acknowledged his effort to renew the method of Socrates, but without giving undue prominence in his philosophy to the new sciences which Aristotle thought had resulted from a like effort in his own works. The coming of Christianity brought new tidings concerning values, concerning the origin, relations, and destiny of men. The Church was established in the Roman Empire three hundred years after the beginning of the Christian era, and Christianity received philosophic systematization in the works of St. Augustine in the course of another hundred years. Augustine had postponed his conversion until he found the instrument for the interpretation of Scripture in the analogical method of Philo and in the rhetorical method of Cicero. Rhetoric, which had become the science of the practical for the Romans, provided the means by which to set forth Christian values, and the use of rhetorical devices disclosed a structure in the philosophy of Plato on which to organize them. The biographies deposited for the canonization of St. Thomas Aquinas, fifty years after his death, stressed the novelty of his philosophy and of the arguments which he brought to the exposition and defense of Christian truths. During the thirteenth century the philosophic works of Aristotle had become available again in the West, and Aquinas's great achievement was to have reconciled the vast corpus of that scientific doctrine and the subtleties of that scientific method with the body of Christian theology and to have saved Christian theology from the dangers of contradiction and heresy which followed from the similarities of Augustinism to Averroistic Aristotelianism. With the beginnings of modern science in the seventeenth century, philosophers renewed their efforts to apply the scientific method to the problems of man: Hobbes was convinced that the science of politics began with his treatise *De Cive;* Descartes, Spinoza, and Locke conceived ethics to be the central trunk of the tree of philosophy and sought, in varying ways, to formulate a science of human behavior; Hume took new inspiration from Newton in his inquiries concerning human understanding and concerning the principles of morals. Kant thought of Copernicus when he sought an analogy to explain the revolution he had worked by making man the center of his philosophy; and John Dewey devoted a great part of his intellectual energy to bringing the method of science to bear on human affairs and on human actions, thinking that in so doing he had accomplished a second Copernican revolution based on the experimental method, not by reorienting the world to the knower, but by indicating the possibility of "naturalizing" knowledge in the life of society.

At each step the novelty is the same; it is the use of science and knowledge—and usually of a specific method which is presented as scientific and practical—for the achievement, preservation, and understanding of values. Yet what is discovered at each step is different, and the discovery not only affects the whole of what is viewed as reality and the whole of what is accepted as knowledge, but also reveals without need of further inquiry the errors of other methods and the illusions of other discoveries. The history of discoveries in philosophy is self-rectifying, for the new truth can seldom be expressed without excursions into a new interpretation of the history of philosophy, of the insights and inadequacies of previous philosophers, of their anticipations of the truth, their tangential excursions into unreal problems which can henceforth be disregarded, and their misguided commitment to false distinctions which delayed the use of the true scientific method and the discovery of the truth. We have made progress in the development of sciences of man and of society, but we have found no means of applying science, even the new "science of values," to human actions even in problems which involve the use of the sciences and which reflect the effect of science on civilization and behavior. We have made progress in the study of values and of their cultural embodiments and interrelations, but we have found no means of making explicit and effective the underlying common values which would save values from the relativism into which they fall when they are naturalized and localized in cultures. The philosophic dimension of this practical dilemma is the inability to relate novelties in their multiplicity to what is constant and common in them—the novelties of the discoveries and principles of successive and contemporary philosophers, the novelties of the discoveries and values of successive and coexistent communities, and the novelties of the discoveries and methods of successive and interdependent sciences.

The philosophic problem of discovery is, in the retrospect of history no less than in the contemporaneous societies of men and the interrelations of knowledge, an old problem which has been discussed under many guises—it is the problem of the one and the many, or the problem of the impact of external influence or change on knowledge and values, or the problem of the application of science to the study of man, society, and human behavior. All of these aspects are present in any instance of philosophic discovery, and a place must be made for them in the execution of the modest task that has been assigned to me of analyzing the circumstances and content of the flash of insight which might be called a discovery in the development of my own philosophic attitude. The statement of the formal aspect of the problem of discovery in its numerous ramifications serves as a massive background against which to trace, and perhaps to lose, the peculiarities of one series of psychological occurrences. That background may be particularized to the stages of my own development by differentiating the four senses of philosophy, for the moment of discovery which I propose to describe is one which I would relate particularly with the emergence in my experience of philosophy in its fourth sense. I had evolved a complete philosophy in the first sense, as a personal expression, at the age of twenty. Indeed, I have never since been able to construct a scheme of solutions of problems, old and new, nearly so complete, certain, or systematic. It had several characteristics which seemed to me important in a philosophy: it made use of the latest advances in the sciences, and particularly in psychology and sociology; it was expressed in a technical language, elaborated at crucial points in a mathematical symbolism, part of which I had borrowed from respected sources and part of which I had invented; it was organized in a system in which the principles were clearly stated and the operations formalized; it had practical applications; and, what was most important, it could be applied to any field of philosophy or to any other subject matter without the need of much effort to become familiar with the intricacies of the subject matter or its problems.

The completeness and attraction of this philosophy as a mode of self-expression were badly damaged by contact with philosophy in its second sense, in which it serves as an instrument to treat problems in the specific forms which they assume in times, and places, and circumstances, and with philosophy in its third sense, in which it makes use of the methods and the accomplishments of science to adapt itself as a form of knowledge to its problems. I discovered, as one step of this transition, that a philosophy is not made practical by the enunciation or the analysis of values and the concomitant criticism of present practices and alternative doctrines: solutions of practical problems are grounded in the situation but are justified by the values they achieve rather than by the opportunity, and they are dependent on the analysis of values that realize actual potentialities. I made the second step by discovering that a philosophy is not made scientific by professing admiration for the scientific method and by aping the technicalities of scientific formulation: achievement and failure in science both share these accidental qualities, and the application of the scientific method consists rather in the attainment of new insights, the discovery of means of validating them, and the inventive exploration of consequences that follow from them. Accompanying these two steps, but scarcely distinguishable from them as a third step, was the discovery that I had read the great philosophers with something less than intellectual ingenuity or sensitive insight, as functions of my own limited point of view rather than as presentations of problems, to be considered in their own right before being dismantled to solve my problems, or as constructions of proof whose grounds and inferences might have criteria other than the commonplaces and rules of operation engrained in my habits and elaborated in my philosophic preferences.

I attached little importance to these steps at the time they were taken, if indeed I was aware of them. They coincided with, if they were not part of, my formal education in philosophy. They may have left traces in my examinations, essays, and theses, but they were not relevant to any of the questions that tested my knowledge or to the contribution to knowledge which I was certified to have made in satisfying the conditions for the doctorate. The problem of the one and the many took concrete form for me in the teaching of two men during my work at Columbia University, and the crossing of their influence was a greater educational force than the teaching of either alone could have been, even if I had been more attentive to what each had said and more conscious than I was, at the time, of its significance. Frederick J. E. Woodbridge stressed with subtle insight and ingenious dialectic the structure of intelligibility in the world. Ideas, he taught, are not inventions constructed by the mind, but discoveries forced upon us by compelling realities whose natures are basically intelligible. Being has intimate relations with being understood, and the fundamental problem of philosophy is not how something nonrational becomes intelligible but how mind is related to many minds. John Dewey, when he returned from China and Japan in 1920, applied his experience and his reflections to the construction of two courses—one on Types of Philosophic Thought, the other on Types of Logical Theory—which set forth the basis of his philosophy more fully than it has appeared in the many books that he was to write in the succeeding decades. In those courses he dwelled on the term which was to become so important in the development of his logic and his political and social philosophy, and explained his hesitations in choosing it. By "experience," he meant, not a psychological stage nor an epistemological category, but rather the context and diversified circumstances in which problems arise and ideas are developed. If he were to seek a single synonym for what he meant by "experience," he said, he would use the term, "culture." He set himself the task of exploring in nonhistorical but systematic fashion the contacts, shifts, alternations, and equivalences of the problems which had been presented to philosophers by experience in their times and of the means which they had devised to treat them. The solutions, like the problems, found their materials, their forms, and their criteria in the economic, social, and intellectual circumstances in which they were developed. In the teachings of Woodbridge and of Dewey the problem of the one and the many is restated in terms appropriate to the problems of our times—not as a problem of essence and existence, nor as a problem of reality and appearance, but as a problem of truth and modes of formulation. The richness and diversity required by the experience and the problems of our times and suggested by the ramifications and successes of scientific inquiry revealed the tenuousness and poverty of the philosophic principles with which I had been engaged and their inadequacy despite the fact that they required only elaboration and application to yield a fully articulated philosophy.

I have constructed this elaborate background of specifications concerning the nature of discovery in philosophy and concerning the situation in which I found myself in education and experience, not as a dodge by which to avoid the question which I have undertaken to answer—the analysis of the occasion of a sudden flash of insight in philosophy and of the uses to which I have put it—but as an essential preliminary to making any answer to that question intelligible. Graham Wallas, who has devoted a book, *The Art of Thought,* to examining the problem of discovery and related processes in the richer data available in the testimony of great thinkers, finds himself constrained to follow a pattern of four stages, first, the Preparation of materials; second, Incubation; third, Illumination or occurrence of the idea; and, finally, Verification. The testimony that Wallas is able to provide for that stage which is intermediate between the labor of preparatory analysis and the unexplained occurrence of a solution is singularly unenlightening. New ideas came to Helmholtz "particularly readily during the slow ascent of wooded hills on a sunny day." Poincaré made two of his great mathematical discoveries after periods of Incubation, due in one case to his military service as a reservist and in the other case to a journey. Old and familiar ideas which I have searched out or encountered at hazard and new ideas, which have led to the reorganization of familiar materials and to hypotheses that I have tried against the requirements of those materials, have both occurred to me under the same two circumstances —from reading books and from conferring, particularly during the period of my work with Unesco, with people of backgrounds, presuppositions, and cultures different than my own. The occasion which seems to me to have influenced my work in philosophy more than any other was an insight that occurred to me in reading. It was not an experience that led to my conversion to a doctrine expressed or to my elaboration of a belief adumbrated and, indeed, I am embarrassed by the fact that I am not sure, after candid examination of my memories, which of two passages furnished the occasion of the insight. I incline consequently to the hypothesis that it was the conjunction and opposition of the two.

The two passages are in the writings of Cicero and of Plato. I attached little importance to the statement of Cicero when I first read it in the *De Finibus,* since it was obviously false. "'My view then,

Cato,' I proceeded, 'is this, that those old disciples of Plato, Speusippus, Aristotle, and Xenocrates, and afterwards their pupils Polemo and Theophrastus, had developed a body of doctrine that left nothing to be desired either in fullness or finish, so that Zeno [the Stoic] on becoming the pupil of Polemo had no reason for differing either from his master himself or from his master's predecessors.' " This is obviously false, since Aristotle, Plato's pupil, devotes so many arguments to the explicit refutation of his master; since the Academy, Plato's school, runs in its evolution through a whole range of possible doctrines from dogmatic idealism to pragmatic skepticism, and the record of the development of the school shows scarcely a master who agreed with the teachings of his predecessor; since the later Peripatetics were unsubtle and unfaithful Aristotelians; and since the Stoics were engaged in controversies, which shifted front with the successive controversialists, against Peripatetics and against Academics, Old and New. Yet as I read Cicero I became more aware of the full import of his thesis—that all philosophies (except the Epicurean, which is, taken simply, false but which, in so far as it is not false, falls under the same thesis) are particular expressions of the same truth and that, in so far as they succeeded in expressing that truth, they differ only verbally. Similarly I attached little importance to the statement in Plato's *Protagoras* at first, since it was obviously a comic interlude to a serious, though inclusive, discussion. After Protagoras, wearied and numbed by Socrates's questions concerning the practicability of his undertaking to teach civic science, was ready to abandon the discussion, he was persuaded to resume by asking rather than answering questions. He chose to vary the approach to the theme by undertaking the interpretation of a poet, Simonides, who wrote a poem developing the theme that it is hard to be good. When Protagoras had completed his interpretation, Socrates appealed to Prodicus and with his approval employed Prodicus's verbal art of interpreting language to remove the contradictions Protagoras had expounded. Socrates then gave a third interpretation of the poem using the resources of his dialectical method to expose the insufficiencies of both Protagoras's sophistic and Prodicus's semantic interpretations. He reinforced his own conclusion by quoting another, unknown, poet—"the good are sometimes bad and sometimes good." This is a paradox employed humorously to introduce a good Socratic point, that the good have the capacity of becoming bad, but the bad have no capacity whatever for becoming but always remain what they are. Yet, as I read in the Platonic dialogues I found myself modifying the verse of the unknown poet and speculating on the evidence that Plato found in the questions of Socrates and in the doctrines of other philosophers—which he can alternately quote for his purposes or refute—that the true is sometimes false and sometimes true.

Discovery is not the simple fitting, or passive addition, of further items of information to a collection of data or to a structure of theory. The effect of a new insight is to modify the interpretation of facts previously known and to necessitate the adjustment or abandonment of theories previously held. It may be welcomed as a contributing cause to total change and revolution in doctrine and attitude; or it may be admitted reluctantly as a sufficient reason for alteration of the customary and accepted. Reading may lead to discovery when what is read is not at first sight, or fully, credible or when it affords grounds for crediting principles or conclusions at variance with those to which assent had been given. Discovery does not result from reading about facts or discourses which follow from or accord with one's basic beliefs; at most such reading leads to the accretion and substantiation of doctrines and the increase and solidification of schools and sects. I had no great admiration for the philosophy of Cicero, although I was convinced in 1921, when the reading of the *De Finibus* came into conjunction with the reading of the *Protagoras,* that his importance as transmitter of Greek culture to the modern world was underrated today and that, under the influence of distaste for his utilitarian verbalism, the similarity of our own philosophic tendencies to his was overlooked. Plato's influence is more frequently acknowledged by modern philosophers, not always for reasons as good or as eloquently expressed as Whitehead's, but the effect of Platonic doctrines and dialectic is usually rendered in a truncated schema which reduces them to a cautious skepticism, like Cicero's Academicism, or a mystical science, like the organic philosophies of Nicholas of Cusa or Whitehead. I had come to see the merits that could be attributed to pragmatisms and to dialectics, but only by a kind of external and intellectual recognition, for I have never felt attracted to the use of pragmatic principles or dialectical methods, preferring to treat theoretic and practical questions separately rather than to assimilate theory to practice or practice to theory.

The recognition, therefore, that there is a sense in which truth, though one, has no single expression and a sense in which truth, though changeless, is rendered false in the uses to which it is put, was attractive in spite of the fact that it ran counter to my most fundamental convictions at the time. I should have preferred to think of the development of philosophy, as knowledge, as a progressive evolution in which errors were detected and discarded and truths were accumulated and interrelated. I should have preferred to think of the applications of philosophy, in practice, as the use of truths administered as specifics to cure evils and operating in constant fashion in conjunction with constant laws of nature and human nature.

Yet philosophic problems seemed to me to have taken on a new form from the new social, political, and moral problems of our times, and both problems, the philosophic and the practical, required a new philosophic approach. Our philosophic problems have centered, for the decades that have passed since I read Cicero and Plato together, in relativism and anti-intellectualism. In its simple form, relativism is a denial of over-all criteria of values, including truth, apart from the particular circumstances in which particular things are in fact valued; there is, however, a second dimension of relativism, which takes its frame of reference not in the different things men call good because they desire them, but in the different principles of partially developed and partially recognized philosophies which guide men's preferences and actions. The first is a relativism of values, based on the conviction that there is no reason why your good should be my good; the second is a relativism of schools and parties, based on the conviction that no reason is adequate to convince you, whatever its cogency and whatever its pertinence to the good, and errors must be extirpated, therefore, and truth must be advanced, by means other than reason—by propaganda, sophistic, indirection, deceit, slander, fear, and if necessary, suppression, force, and liquidation. In its simple form, anti-intellectualism is a confidence, accompanied by a distrust of analytic statement and rational proof, that sensitivity and good intentions are enough; there is, however, a second stage of anti-intellectualism, in which the distrust of reason, buttressed by reasons, becomes a roundly expressed and argued distress at other men's reasons in the oppositions and intolerances of schools, parties, and sects. The change in these narrowly philosophic problems, which gives them greater importance beyond philosophy than they have ever had before, results from changes in the world situation which makes the relations of peoples, nations, classes, and in general all associations, profoundly philosophic problems. Men of all cultures, of all nations, and of all philosophies have been brought into contacts that affect every aspect of their lives. The values which motivate them are different. Either their different values are different expressions of the same values, in which case values can be differentiated from pseudo-values and truths from errors; or they are irreducibly relative, in which case conflicts among value structures result from, and are resolved by, oppositions of power, and men would prefer to remain neutral to any such conflict unless they are involved, not by reason or conviction, but by interest or force. The statement of this conflict employs reasons and ideals; to judge by the arguments that have been employed to make it clear, the whole tradition of Western thought culminates in the oppositions which now tend to divide all men, and any philosopher may be blamed in those oppositions for the errors to be resisted, or, alternatively, may be praised as a source of truth or a guide for action. Philosophy has entered into a new importance in the ideological conflict, but the use of philosophy is so clouded by ambiguities that the practical relevance of principles and arguments is itself thrown into doubt. We are losing hold of truth because of the variety of ways in which it is expressed, and we are losing confidence in truth because of the degradations to which concepts, which were conceived to express ideals, and statements, which were thought to express truths, are put in their practical uses and manipulations.

I have gone ahead of the story of the flash of insight that came from Cicero and Plato some thirty years ago in order to indicate the significance I was later to attach to it. The steps by which the insight was bodied forth to this broad interpretation from the situation which followed World War I to the situation which developed from World War II were slow and meticulous. If it is true that there is no single statement of the single truth and that any statement of truth, however well articulated and painstakingly verified, is subject to degradation, misinterpretation, and misapplication, it becomes important to distinguish the aspects by which the forms of expression and proof may be differentiated and by which the criteria of continuing validity and value may be applied. Philosophies may be distinguished with respect to four basic differences: philosophers talk about different subject matters; they employ different methods in their treatment of the same or different matters; they base their methods on different assumptions and principles; and they direct their philosophic constructions and speculations to different ends. Once these differences have been elaborated, it is easy to recognize Aristotle's four causes in them; and since Aristotle has been able to find no more than four causes, there was some ground for the presumption that I should encounter no more in the writings of another two thousand years of philosophers. But whereas inquiry into the operation of causes led Aristotle to examine the first principles of being and to develop what was later to be called a metaphysics, inquiry into the operation of causes had apparently started me on an examination of first principles of philosophic discourse and to develop a form of what is now called semantics. If I had unconsciously borrowed the principles of my inquiry from Aristotle, I was committed to using them on a different subject matter.

The changes in the subject matter which philosophers treat supply the most immediately apparent differences among philosophies. It is the source of most of the revolutions proclaimed by philosophers— such as Kant's and Dewey's Copernican revolutions—and it gives to the history of philosophy the appearance of periodization which lead philosophers and historians of some philosophic schools to discover that ages have their characteristic "spirits" or "climates" or "philosophies" and that the history of philosophy follows a cyclical or a cumulative or a rising and falling development. During any given period, philosophers treat in their theories and discussions what may be conceived broadly as the same subject matter, and they differ in the methods they employ, in the principles in which the method is grounded, and in the ends to which it is directed. For all the differences of philosophies, there is a homogeneity in the discussion inasmuch as they raise the same or comparable questions and give different answers to them. When the subject matter changes, due to external influences or to the revolutions of philosophers, the fundamental questions are changed and the problems that were basic and difficult in the previous period become derived and relatively easy to treat as simple consequences or as unreal puzzles, and philosophers in the new tradition may either underline their originality and independence of previous philosophic traditions or their fidelity to the old methods, perennial principles, and traditional purposes which are put to new uses in application to the new problems.

The broad philosophic sense in which philosophers for a time concentrate their attention on the same subject matter is apparent in the distinctions which they make in subject matters at each stage of the discussion. For a time they treat the nature of things as their fundamental concern and make problems of knowledge, action, and expression depend on basic principles of being and becoming, essence and existence, matter and motion. Differences concerning the nature of being lead eventually to such subtle differentiations, such complex interrelations, such massive consequences that philosophers turn in the search for prior questions to an examination of the grounds on which such differences can be simplified and the nature of things can be known and verified. For a time philosophers then seek criteria of knowledge which permit them to treat questions of the nature of things as well as questions of action and expression as consequences of these basic distinctions. But again differences concerning the nature and grounds of knowledge become subtle, massive, and polar, and philosophers turn in an effort to find prior questions to an examination of the means of simplifying such differences and of testing knowledge by the practical consequences to which it leads or by the form of language—scientific proof, practical communication, esthetic construction, spiritual preachment—in which they are set forth. The criteria of the practical and the techniques of verbal analysis, in turn, become involved in ambiguities, uncertainties, and antithetical formalisms, which return philosophers to the expectation that the ends of actions and the meanings and values of symbols must be grounded in the nature of things, and that the fundamental analysis for philosophy must be sought in being, not in knowledge, or action, or statement.

Recognition of the sequence in which philosophers have gone through these stages of reaction a number of times in the history of Western thought does not lead necessarily to a *Geistesgeschichte* or a dialectic according to which ages follow a necessary order of growth and decline, although it does reveal, as would be proper in the inquiry in which I proposed to engage, the grounds on which dialectical philosophies might allege such an order. The richness and diversity of approaches and methods can be distinguished, nonetheless, within each age and can be related to comparable methods, principles, and purposes across the dividing lines of subject matter and problems which separate ages.

Plato, Democritus, Aristotle, and the Sophists, whose lives overlapped, found their philosophic principles in the nature of things: Plato sought the fundamental reality in Ideas; Democritus explained all processes, including the processes of thought, by the motion of atoms; Aristotle professed to avoid reducing things to thoughts or thoughts to things, and constructed a system of sciences adjusted to differences of problems; and Isocrates reduced all theoretic problems to their practical terms and found the true philosophic method in rhetoric. The deaths of Alexander, Aristotle, and Demosthenes within a period of little more than a year marked the end of an epoch. Philosophers for a time thereafter sought their basic principles in the criteria of knowledge, yet Stoics and Epicureans, Academics and Skeptics derived inspiration for this new task in the earlier philosophies. Epicurus modified the doctrine of Democritus in the construction of his Canon to set forth and employ the criteria of knowledge and to make clear the inadequacies and irrelevancies of formal logic; the Academics professed to follow Plato in the sequences of their skeptical and dogmatic schools; the Stoics adapted something of the method and terminology of Aristotle to what they conceived to be the true development of Plato in the elaboration of a propositional logic; and the Peripatetics became scholars and technical scientists. Under the spreading Roman rule, philosophers took their beginnings in the consideration of how men talk and how men act, yet they appropriated to that analysis the doctrines of Stoics, Epicureans, Academics, and Skeptics. Cicero constructed a practical philosophy under the inspiration of Socrates and Isocrates by wedding wisdom and eloquence and by reconciling the differences of schools; Sextus Empiricus attacked dogmatism in all the sciences by analysis of the signs employed in constructing the sciences; rhetoric developed in many forms culminating under the Empire in a New Sophistic; and Platonism emerged under the same circumstances in a New Platonism.

Theory and practice, principles and experience, values and circumstances, all contributed to these successive changes of subject matter and to the modification which the oppositions of philosophers underwent in successive applications. The coming of Christianity affected the subject matter of philosophy in all these respects: it supplied new data and new tidings relevant to the nature, origin, and destiny of man; it suggested new principles for the organization of these and like data and provided new ends to which to orient life and knowledge; it first opposed and resisted and then appropriated and modified the methods of the philosophers. In the East, the development of a Christian philosophy took a theoretic turn in dogmatic disputes concerning the true doctrine; in the West, under the influence of Cyprian, Ambrose, and Augustine, it took a practical turn in the organization of the Church and in its establishment in the context of the Empire. Western Christianity found in the writings of St. Augustine a complete philosophy which was to continue to influence the whole course of Christian thought; Boethius professed to depart in no respect from the doctrine of Augustine, but he found it desirable to restate its arguments to bring forth the grounds and criteria on which it is established, and he furnished the basic texts which set Christians discussing the problem of the universal and the consolations of philosophy; Cassiodorus restated the liberal arts, treating the arts of the trivium as verbal, in relation to Christian doctrine, and Isidore of Seville reduced knowledge to an encyclopedic compendium organized according to the etymologies of the basic terms employed in stating it.

Philosophy took new life and a new subject matter from the practical problems of politics treated in terms of the liberal arts in the court of Charlemagne and from the practical problems of canon law treated in like terms in the court of Charles the Bald. These led to problems of criteria and sources of knowledge and action which threatened during the tenth and eleventh centuries to set theology and philosophy in opposition, but the method which was to be called the "Scholastic method" and which moved from canon law to theology and thence to philosophy provided a means for their reconciliation by assembling the opposed answers to common questions and by examining their differences and, in so doing, it set men discussing once more the problem of the universal. John of Salisbury, in the twelfth century, sought escape from these problems in a humanistic pragmatic philosophy, modeled on the Ciceronean Academicism and constructed in the light of the difficulties which his master, Pierre Abelard, encountered in the construction of a nominalistic dialectic. The translation of the works of Aristotle during the twelfth and early thirteenth century created a sharp break in the development of Christian philosophy by providing a new subject matter organized in a vast scientific corpus and a new method used in the treatment of that subject matter and expounded in Aristotle's treatises on logic. Roger Bacon, Alexander of Hales, Albertus Magnus, Bonaventura, and Thomas Aquinas, among many other writers, labored to reconcile this material to the doctrines of Christianity and to extricate the doctrines of Augustine from the consequences of its similarities and antitheses to Arabic Aristotelianism. All the varieties of methods found development and application during the thirteenth century, and the earlier fourteenth century turned, under the influence of Duns Scotus, from the complexities of metaphysics and theology to questions of criteria of knowledge by which to mediate those differences. The latter half of the

fourteenth century and the Renaissance, in turn, abandoned epistemology to construct terminalistic logics, such as occupied Ockham,
rhetorical and literary philosophies in forms as different as those of
Ramus and Nizolius, practical philosophies such as Machiavelli
elaborated, and in the interplay of methods and principles new interpretations of man's end and of the means by which to achieve it were
sought in the Reformation and Counter-Reformation.

The development of modern science again provided a new subject
matter for philosophy. Even before the seventeenth century, writers
like Telesio and Campanella found the bases for their philosophies in
the new science; and the philosophies of Bacon, Hobbes, Descartes,
Spinoza, Leibnitz, Locke, Berkeley, and Hume are inseparable from
efforts to state and develop the new methods of science and to apply
them to philosophic problems and to speculations concerning man.
Although many of these philosophers developed their methods by
tracing the origin and relations of ideas, by distinguishing simple
ideas, complex ideas, and modes, or by seeking clear, distinct, and
adequate ideas, Kant was correct in recognizing that their philosophies were oriented to the nature of things—to God, nature, and the
self, to thought and extension, to space and the motions of things—and
in claiming the distinction for himself of having reoriented philosophy
to man and to the forms of thought. The nineteenth century labored
with the criteria and limits of thought and with the ramifications of
philosophical anthropology and epistemology; and we have rounded
the turn, once more in the twentieth century, by reacting against ideal-
isms to seek the subject matter of philosophy in action, experience,
and the patterns of cultures and in symbols, communication, and the
demonstrations of science.

Even so cursory a view of the history of subject matters of philosophic discussion throws some light on the nature of the discovery
that came to me from the pages of Cicero and Plato, for it explains
the uneasy similarities of our own philosophic preoccupations to those
of the Roman, the Carolingian, and the Renaissance periods. Cicero
was engaged on a similar subject matter when he found a single truth
differently expressed in the different philosophies, and Socrates's interlude with the Sophists in explanation of the poetic insight, that the

good are sometimes bad and sometimes good, is closer to the doctrine of the New Academy, which Cicero professed, than to the loftier reaches of the Platonic doctrine of Ideas. Moreover, it explains why any application that I might seek to make of Aristotle's four causes would lead me, if I was sensitive to subject matter of my contemporaries in philosophy, to the development of a semantics as a propaedeutic to metaphysical or epistemological inquiries.

The differences of the methods employed by philosophers are apparent in the differentiation of the subject matters which they treat in successive periods. These differences are stated in a vast variety of ways, usually in polemical discussions in which all other methods are contrasted to the one employed in the statement. It early became apparent to me that some schematism must be developed which would permit the comparison of methods without distortion by the peculiarities of any one method, if the sense and the extent to which different philosophies express an identical or similar truth and the sense and the extent to which they slip into error and perversion were to be revealed objectively and neutrally. In the course of searching for such a schematism I became convinced that a formal structure would have to be found which would at one and the same time guarantee that the methods distinguished were mutually exclusive, exhaustive of the possibilities of methodological difference, and the source of all the subdivisions and secondary variations of method, and also that they were subject to statement, in the schematism, indifferently in equivalent though different forms according to all the methods. The basis for such a schematism must have some relation to the large structures which appear as philosophies are developed according to their appropriate methods. I found in a classification of these structures under four heads the beginnings of a schematism which satisfied the criteria I had set up.

There are, in the first place, philosophies which begin with the conviction that the whole, however the "whole" is conceived—the universe, the whole of knowledge or experience, the whole man, the whole of civilization, the whole of values, of modes of expression, or of means and potentialities of being, thought, action, and statement—cannot be treated adequately in terms of its parts. No independent entities, ideas, values, or actions are conceivable or possible in these philosophies, but the problem of philosophy is to trace the lines by which everything is related to everything else in being and operation, in knowledge and impulse, in value and implication. Philosophers who develop this conviction in varying ways frequently profess to use the dialectical method, and I decided to examine the method common to all such philosophies under the rubric "dialectic." There are, in the second place, and at the opposite extreme, philosophies which undertake the enterprise of seeking least parts from which to construct those portions of knowledge or reality that are now accessible to man, while postponing the delineation of the whole, except in so far as its nature is predetermined by the assumption that it can be treated by such construction, until knowledge is available for such reformulation. The least parts are sometimes sought in things (such as atoms whose characteristics, motions, and combinations will then explain all phenomena), sometimes in thought (such as simple ideas, whose characteristics, modifications, and combinations will then provide the criteria of certainty and probability and the method by which to proceed by least steps through the long chains of reasoning that constitute science), and sometimes in symbols or signs (such as the undefined terms and rules of combination which serve to construct languages and which provide the method by which ultimately to deduce all sciences from a single set of principles). In the phase in which these philosophies sought their principles in material atoms, they were criticized by dialecticians as "logistic," and in the phase in which they used symbols as principles, their proponents tended to describe the method as logistic, and I therefore decided to use that "logistic" as the rubric under which to study all such methods. There are, in the third place, philosophies which are midway between these two extreme assumptions, inasmuch as the philosophers who engage in philosophic speculation of this kind are equally dubious of the possibility and desirability of basing a philosophy on knowledge of the whole or of the least part, and they engage instead in the construction of a variety of sciences adapted to a variety of problems, subject matters, and purposes. These philosophers are inclined to treat philosophic method as "inquiry" and to orient philosophic inquiry to "problems," and I therefore studied the methods they employed in order to characterize the "problematic" method. In addition to philosophies oriented to the whole and to internal relations within it, and philosophies oriented to the part and to combinations and constructions which they make possible or explain, and philosophies oriented to problems and their resolution without reference to holistic or atomic principles, there are, in the fourth place, philosophies which oppose to all types of theoretic construction the conviction that philosophy and knowledge should seek criteria in particular and practical consequences in action. The names historically used by the proponents of this method have all taken on pejorative senses as a result of the attacks of more theoretic philosophers—as "sophistic" retains the sense Plato and Aristotle gave it and "academic" (apart from the new layer of meaning derived from association with modern schools) retains the sense Augustine and Duns Scotus gave it—and I therefore used the term, "operationalism," which is somewhat broader in its common use, to designate this method the "operational method."

The broad characteristics of these four methods and their adaptation to the subject matters discussed by philosophers in successive ages are apparent throughout the history of philosophy despite the great variety of forms which each of the methods assumes. The dialectical method is analogical: terms properly assume a variety of meanings in the course of their use even in scientific demonstration, and the development of dialectic has an apparent unity which permits later dialecticians to recognize earlier uses of dialectic, and indeed of any other method, as preparations for, and dialectically explained antecedents to, the forms of dialectic later practiced. Moreover, the differences of subject matter which separate the ages, from the point of view of other methods, are only apparent, not real, from the point of view of dialectic, for the processes of things and the processes of thoughts, and *a fortiori* the processes of action and statement, all reflect the same dialectical pattern, and history is intimately related to, if not identical with, proof. The logistic method, on the contrary, is literal and univocal: terms should be defined unambiguously and should retain, throughout proof and communication, the same meanings. The changes of subject matter which separate the ages separate the successive uses of the logistic method by sharp differences, for the philosopher must decide, since the method depends on the combination of least parts, whether his least parts are to be atoms, simple ideas, or symbols and, once he has chosen one, he can state and explain phenomena relative to the others in its basic terms, and his method consists in one of the many forms of the "combinatory art." The problematic method depends, like the logistic method, on the establishment of univocal terms and literal meanings; but, since there are many problems and many sciences, any important term has many meanings which must be distinguished before the proper meaning is used in the proper place, while the interrelations among these meanings is established in basic sciences, like metaphysics, by means of analogies among meanings reminiscent of the dialectic method. The differences of subject matter discussed is reflected in the problematic method by differences of the analyses and the sciences taken to be "architectonic" in determining the spread and interrelation of meanings—sometimes metaphysics or epistemology, sometimes "politics" or semantics, sometimes sociology or the study of humanistic aspects of cultures and arts. The operational method, like dialectic, is not constrained to literal or single meanings in its use of terms, but unlike dialectic its meanings are imposed either by arbitrary decision of the user of the method or by irrational determination of the operation of circumstances: for the agent who has power to control what is done, meanings are what he decides they should be; otherwise, they are determined by chance or fortune to which the practitioner of the operational method learns to adapt his actions and meanings.

Not only may philosophic methods be described in terms of their use of symbols in application to the changes of subject matter in philosophy, which had early forced themselves on my attention as one of the means by which philosophies are differentiated from each other, but methods are also distinct from each other in the relations between science and action, theory and practice, which they entail. The relation of knowledge to action had seemed to me to be one of the outstanding problems of our times, and it was one of the problems which had led me to the inquiry concerning the relations among philosophies. There are four possible relations between theory and practice, and the fact that one of these relations followed from each of the methods I had sketched seemed to me partial confirmation of the soundness and relevance of my schematism. If, with the dialectician all things are to be explained in their mutual relations in a single whole, there is no difference between theory and practice. Dialecticians have repeatedly urged that identity and have criticized practice separated from theory and theory separated from practice throughout the history of dialectic. This at least is common, among all the important differences that separate them, between Plato's use of Socrates's principle that virtue is knowledge and the Marxist use of the science of the history of society as the prototype of all science and the source of all action. The operationalist's conviction that theory should be tested by practice and that theories without consequences in action are trivial has a similar effect of identifying theory and practice but for opposite reasons, since theory is then reduced to practice whereas practice reaches its fullest possibilities and clearest explanations on the background of an over-all theory in dialectic. The other two methods distinguish knowledge and action, theory and practice, but in two different ways. For the logistic method, theory is established in science while action finds its motive and cause in some impulse, nonrational in foundation and noncognitive in operation. Science and action are therefore mutually exclusive: it is possible to have a science of all varieties of processes, including the operations and actions of men, but the motives which lead a man to action, even the action of engaging in scientific inquiry, are found in passion, habituation, accident, as well as in reason. One modern form of this distinction has become popular among philosophers who practice the logistic method in the distinction between the language of science, which is cognitive, and the language of ethics or esthetics, which is noncognitive, inasmuch as it is persuasive or emotive. For the problematic method, on the other hand, the distinction between theory and practice does not lead to the conclusion that demonstration is scientific and action nonscientific, but rather to the conclusion that, since methods vary with the variation of problems, the method of the theoretic sciences is distinct from the method of the practical sciences. Both methods, the logistic and the problematic, lead to the conclusion that the scientific method should be employed more than it is in the treatment of the problems of human action; but in the logistic method, that conviction leads to the search for a science—like psychology, sociology, or anthropology—which uses the same scientific method as the natural sciences, to cure the tensions, fears, misapprehensions, and mental illnesses which prevent men from acting as they should, whereas in the problematic method, the same conviction leads to the search, avoiding the dangerous analogy of the natural sciences, for a science which will effect communication among men as the necessary preliminary to agreement concerning the use of the technical processes of engineering and the applied sciences and the application of the conclusions of the pure sciences.

These distinctions in the field of the practical brought to my attention a homogeneity between the dialectical and the operational methods, on the one hand, and the logistic and the problematic methods, on the other, which goes beyond questions of the relation of theory and practice to questions of "scientific method" in the various senses proper to each approach. To signify these similarities I found it desirable to invent two terms: "holoscopic" to indicate the respects in which dialectical and operational methods "view" problems in their relation to some "whole," and "meroscopic" to signify the two ways in which the logistic and problematic methods "view" problems relative to the "parts" from which the whole is constructed or to the circumstances which determine the occurrence and the character of the problem.

Two more differences—differences of principles or assumptions and differences of ends or purposes—enter into the differentiation of the vast number of philosophies which have been developed in the course of the history of thought. What I have said concerning the differences of subject matters and methods is sufficient to indicate the character of the inquiry in which I engaged as a result of the discovery to which I was led by Cicero and Plato, and whereas the additional differences of principles and ends are essential to account for the relations and oppositions among philosophies in their theoretic development and in their practical application, to set forth still more differences at this point would needlessly complicate the exposition of what is involved in a moment of discovery. One question which occurs at almost any stage of the elaboration of that discovery, however, must be answered if what I have said is not to be reduced to an obvious and simple-minded parologism. If the basic problem of this semantic investigation of the relation of meanings in different philosophies involves the classification of all possible methods, what method is used in that classification? If the classification is exhaustive of all methods, must not the method of classification be one of the methods classified, and is not the inquiry itself, therefore, involved in the relativities and distortions it seeks to avoid and to resolve?

The criteria which I set forth to govern the construction of the schematism of methods supplies the answer to these questions. The schematism must be neutral, not in the sense of being conceived and stated apart from the methods it treats, but in the sense of being susceptible of statement without distortion in each of the methods. The use of the method in the formulation of the schematism will, therefore, differ from the use of the method in the resolution of practical and philosophic problems. It is possible to examine the problem of the relation of methods dialectically, operationally, logistically, and problematically, taking as data the doctrines of philosophers—professional philosophers and also that much larger group of philosophers who simply relate what they think, say, and do to contexts larger than the immediate consequences they anticipate or encounter. This is a problem in what I came to call "historical" semantics, and there is no reason why the differences of meanings encountered in the course of discussion or history should not be subject to such statement in any of the methods. Once attention is turned from the varieties of philosophies as the subject matter of inquiry and once one of the methods is employed on the subject matter of philosophy adapted to the times and the preferences of the philosopher, the use of the method results in the development of a particular philosophy and in that philosophy particular meanings are determined and assigned to terms, which are to be preferred over other possible meanings. This is a problem in what I came to call "philosophical" semantics. The course of inquiry which I followed and the exposition which I have just given of it, thus, employ the problematic method. There is no reason why one should not be led from this problematic statement of the differences of method to the choice of the dialectical, the operational, or the logistic method as best adapted to the solution of some problems or as the preferable method for philosophy in general. There is likewise no reason why the schematic differences of method might not be restated dialectically, operationally, or logistically with no more pre-judgment or distortion, than in the statement I have given, in which, for example, prior to commitment to a philosophy which fixes its meaning, each of the four meanings of the "practical" is equally defensible and equally fruitful of consequences. I have made such a translation of the schematism into the other methods elsewhere, but, for our purposes today, indication of its possibility is sufficient to clarify the assumptions on which my analysis proceeded. Once the choice of the method is made, after the propaedeutic analysis of meanings in "historical" semantics, one is constrained by the "philosophic" semantics determined by one's assumptions to one set of meanings for all fundamental terms—for "cause" or "democracy" or "imagination"—and even the fullest tolerance of intellectual differences is no justification for restraining the impulse to demonstrate that other meanings are absurd or impractical in the treatment of problems to which the method is committed.

I have explained the discovery to which I was led from reading in Cicero and Plato by setting forth, in perhaps excessive detail, distinctions in the subject matters and methods of philosophers, and insights concerning these distinctions, to which the discovery led. I have explained the mechanisms in which I later encased the insight, not the insight itself, and since I sought those mechanisms in formal distinctions among philosophies and among sciences, I am afraid that I have given the discovery itself a formalistic and historical turn. The data on which the insight was employed were the statements, preferably the well ordered or scientific statements made by different men and in different circumstances, but form and history tend to conceal the purpose of the inquiry, which was philosophic, and to leave wholly out of account the novelty which the method introduces into the problems and applications of philosophy. "Historical" semantics derives its distinctions from history and provides means by which to read intellectual history more intelligently and more profitably; it leads from history to insight into the nature and the interrelations of the sciences and into the effectiveness and varieties of expressions of values. But the characteristic result of historical semantics, to which my attention was turned from my first efforts to treat the problem of varying meanings and varying proofs, is to be found in application to new problems of philosophy, which are the mark and product of our times.

Philosophy is not only a form of knowledge; it is also an expression of cultures. In a world in which many distinct and divergent cultures are in unavoidable contact as a result of the progress of science, the temptation is natural to seek solutions to the resulting tensions among peoples by the construction and use of another science. The application of any form of science chosen for this purpose conceals one form of philosophy, and the opposition to any such program is not an opposition to science, but the mark and indication of a whole range of philosophic problems which are prior to commitment to action or to grounds for action. They involve a preliminary study of the relations of cultures as expressions of values, divergent in form but possibly identical with each other in fundamental character, which reproduce, when they are stated formally, differences on which philosophers have been engaged ever since Socrates brought philosophy down from the skies. In those relations—whether they are stated theoretically or evolved practically in the course of action—real differences are confounded with differences which are only in expression and in approach. In the emerging community of the world the first problem of philosophy—the new metaphysics or at least the new prolegomenon to all future metaphysics—will expound the sense in which truth is one, despite the multiplicity of the forms of its expression, and the sense in which what is on some grounds or in some circumstances true is at other times false and dangerous.

XI

THINKERS WHO INFLUENCED ME

BY

HAROLD TAYLOR

I share with Immanuel Kant only one philosophical attribute. We were both awakened by David Hume. What followed after the awakening is another matter, a matter connected with the quality, range, and depth of a philosophical mind which turned the course of Western philosophy in a new direction. For my part, I am content to say humbly that I have continued to learn from great philosophical minds other than Kant, to accept the influence of radical empiricism, and to enjoy learning from the philosophers of organism, principally from Bergson, from James, from Whitehead, from Dewey.

I can think of no precise moment when the impact of Hume's ideas suddenly or dramatically changed the course of my thinking. The most I can do is to describe as accurately as my memory allows some intellectual experiences which my colleagues here today may be interested in comparing with their own.

I come therefore under false pretenses; my instances are not dramatic, my experience is not unusual, and my conclusions, although of course sound, true, and good, are not of wide philosophical significance. I am merely a case study of one kind of person with one kind of philosophy. I might add however that this kind of philosophy is true, and that any intelligent person must agree with it.

When I first read philosophy I read it as the history of certain ideas. I assumed that the ideas began with Plato, who gave intellectual currency to the basic philosophical questions, and then were carried through the minds of others, century after century, in regular order, like annual reports or like monthly issues of a magazine. The ideas themselves were sometimes interesting, often not. They were collected into various systems, some starting at one point, some at another, and were ordered logically according to certain rules upon which everyone agreed. A variety of systems had appeared, all of them justifiable, all of them, in a sense, equal, and the role of the student-philosopher was to recognize the systems by the names of the philosophers who had made them. These ideas were not to be dealt with in terms of their ultimate value, their validity, their truth, or their contribution to human understanding. They were not to be criticized from a single point of view, but to be understood, remembered, and known. Those systems which had appeared fairly recently were to be studied last, if at all, and then only with a view to locating them in the tradition from which they came. The master of all philosophers was Hoffding who had the whip hand because of his knack of putting every philosopher in his proper place through his formidable works in the history of philosophy. His erudition enabled him to dispose accurately of all philosophical questions. Professor Hoffding thus enabled the student-philosopher to answer questions. The fact that these were questions which only people like Hoffding would ask, seemed perfectly natural to me at the time.

Simultaneously with this philosophical reading, I was concerned to read literature from the same general point of view. Although at the age of eight I had decided to be a writer, largely under the influence of Robert Louis Stevenson and *Treasure Island,* the bulk of my reading was conducted under the auspices of educational authorities who had clear ideas concerning the need for covering ground, and I discovered that for purposes of becoming educated in literature, it was often better not to read the original authors but to go straight to the heart of the matter by reading Legouis and Cazamian's *History of English Literature,* or some equally competent text in the field. In this manner I received a degree of attention, honor, and scholastic distinction sufficient to encourage both the educational authorities and myself to go ahead with my work, and at the same time, saved many hours of drudgery which might have come from dealing with the actual materials of literature and philosophy. This left me free for other pursuits which seemed important at the time, including athletics, music, poetry, novels, youth, life, and the general pursuit of happiness.

None of these activities, intellectual or otherwise, were sufficiently absorbing or meretricious to deaden completely a latent interest in books and ideas. My difficulty was that none of the books or ideas by which this latent interest was aroused had anything to do with the philosophers and writers I was officially called upon to study. Although I kept this as a species of guilty secret, it was not until the formal aspect of my philosophical development had been certified and guaranteed by various institutions, and I had been called upon to teach what I had learned, that I realized that it was possible to hold a philosophical position of one's own by which other positions might be judged, or that the illicit interest which I had in what can only be called a philosophy of the present was in fact legitimate and in theory respectable.

I now come to my first remarkable experience. Consider the following passage from David Hume. It is from the *Treatise,* and is drawn from that section in which Hume traces the argument which led to his conclusions about the function of imagination in the formation of belief.

> After the most accurate and exact of my reasonings,
> I can give no reason why I should assent to it; . . .

I had not noticed this passage before, although I had read it several times, and, I have reason to believe, had commented on it successfully. I realized for the first time that I had been philosophically cheated, that I had been playing an elaborate game in which the rules had never been explained to me, and that the logical structure of language, concepts, ideas, and the rules for dealing with that structure, had no basis in my personal reality. I had never asked myself why I assented to any conclusion, nor how any claim for truth could actually be justified. I read on:

I can give no reason why I should assent to it; and feel nothing but a *strong* propensity to consider objects *strongly* in that view, under which it appears to me. Experience is a principle which instructs me in the several conjunctions of objects for the past. Habit is another principle, which determines me to expect the same for the future; and both of them conspiring to operate upon the imagination, make me form certain ideas in a more intense and lively manner, than others, which are not attended with the same advantages. Without this quality, by which the mind enlivens some ideas beyond others (which seemingly is so trivial and so little founded on reason) we could never assent to any argument nor carry our view beyond those few objects, which are present to our senses. Nay, even to those objects, we cou'd never attribute any existence, but what was dependent on the senses; and must comprehend them entirely in that succession of perceptions which constitutes our self or person. Nay, farther, even with relation to that succession, we cou'd only admit of those perceptions which are immediately present to our consciousness; nor cou'd those lively images, with which the memory presents us, be ever receiv'd as true pictures of past perceptions. The memory, senses, and understanding, are therefore all of them founded on the imagination or the vivacity of our ideas.

The abyss had opened. Systems of thought were swallowed up. Aristotelian psychology disappeared in the void. Platonic forms went heavenward in a swarm. Rational absolutes scudded across in thin vaporous streaks. Realism and nominalism tumbled in. Descartes, who had peered briefly into the chasm and then drawn back was lost to human view. Academic philosophy, nineteenth century idealism, the pre-Socratics, the Scholastics, the Cambridge Platonists, the metaphysicians all rolled together over the edge. All that remained was a cluster of hardy philosophers with heads strong enough to view the abyss without dizziness, a few shrieks of delight from the logical positivists, a hoot of derision from Bertrand Russell, and I saw the beckoning hand of William James and his friends.

Apart from this, nothing much happened. From that point on I was lost to the blandishments of radical empiricism. The implications of Hume's philosophy became clearer as I read again the *Treatise* and the *Enquiry*, this time with a sense of excitement and discovery. I discovered that I disagreed with those who had given Hume his place in history of philosophy as a skeptic who destroyed the possibility of rational certainty, as a man who employed the "fallacy of simple location," who destroyed the logical construct of the self, who atomized experience into discrete units, who made necessary the *a priori* of Kant. It seemed to me that Hume was a naturalist and very sensible about it. He refused to accept the conventional eighteenth century assumptions about the reason as a separate entity, or the idea of rational certainty as defined by Descartes. His analysis of experience had shown that there is not a subjective and objective world or mind and matter as the classical philosophers had held. If you begin with these worlds, Hume was saying, you will find yourself unable to prove the existence of an external world. Rather, you must begin with the experience of an individual in relation to a world whose prior existence must be assumed but cannot be proven. You then find certain psychological facts concerning unavoidable intellectual habits, the imagination, the memory, the reason, which underlie the process of concept-making itself, and thus underlie logical constructs and logical principles. I decided that Hume was concerned not so much with the denial of the possibility of human knowledge as with the refutation of that philosophy which spins the world out of one's head instead of spinning one's head out of the world.

But more important than these particular conclusions was the fact that I had found a sense of philosophical identity. I discovered that it was not necessary to accept systems of ideas at their own valuation, and that each person capable of any degree of sustained thought could, within the limits of that degree, develop a philosophical position of his own by which to understand himself, his world, and other philosophers. It was this discovery, which came not on a single day, or through a single experience, but through a slow saturation with the ideas of naturalism which I had found one day in Hume, which marked a turning point in the development of a philosophical position of my own.

The intellectual surroundings for this process of development were fortunate—fortunate, that is, for naturalism. The liberal atmosphere of teaching and learning which existed on the campus of the University of Wisconsin was one in which young people, whether students or teachers, could find stimulation and congenial intellectual company. My colleagues in philosophy, led by Max Otto, had formed one of the most vigorous and creative groups of teachers of philosophy of any university in the country. Professor Otto's leadership was one which focussed our attention on two things, the development in our students of philosophical insight, and the development in ourselves of a serious concern for the relation of thought to action, of philosophy to education, of ideals to reality. We represented a variety of points of view as we worked together, but whatever phase of the work we undertook, we were given an opportunity to express that point of view in our teaching and to enrich our own research by relating it to the teaching itself. For me, this was a liberating and rewarding experience which I was fortunate to have had, and whatever merit there may be in the educational ideas I am now engaged in expressing through my work as a college administrator is based upon the learning experience of those days with my colleagues in philosophy and the privilege of teaching in an institution where new ideas were encouraged and liberalism was an indigenous philosophy which permeated the social and intellectual atmosphere.

I would now like to leave David Hume and his educational effects to go back to another set of experiences which seem to me to have had some importance in influencing my thinking. I have always had the advantage of never having had money, along with the additional advantage of not having considered this extraordinary. In my early years, nothing much had ever been said in my presence about the struggle between the haves and the have-nots, and although I knew of the existence of poverty, social distress, unemployment, and social tensions, I had never considered this theoretically as a struggle between classes. To me it had always seemed possible for a person with enough energy and willingness to work hard to make enough money to survive. I believe I can point to the exact time when I realized that this was not true and to the time when I discovered I was politically and socially naive and innocent.

The experience I recall most vividly occurred in 1936 in Trafalgar Square in London. As a student at the University of London, I was absorbed in the study of eighteenth century philosophy and literature, and had a daily route which took me to the British Museum, to the university, and home again, without many other excursions into the political and social situation of England in 1936. I had, however, read newspaper accounts of a group of Welsh miners who objected to the means test which the Conservative government had imposed to decide whether or not workers were entitled to the dole. I had read that a group of 150 of them had set out on foot from Wales to present themselves at the Prime Minister's residence in London to protest. In each town and village through which they marched they were put up by the local residents, and represented in their own way a symbol of social protest by the economically deprived who were victims of a social system. They were willing to work but could not be employed, and they resented bitterly being considered as testable material for the governmental process.

I was in Trafalgar Square when they marched through a mass of London citizens on their way to the Prime Minister. I can never forget the look of their faces as they marched through the square. Their faces were drawn, their eyes were bitter, and the set of their bodies as they marched showed a self-confidence and a sense of purpose which frightened me and suddenly opened up a whole new area of undeveloped knowledge, emotion, and anxiety. The speeches which their leaders made to the crowded square were the most exciting and vigorous I had ever heard.

From that point on, the superficial political and social knowledge which I possessed as a student of philosophy took on a new meaning, and I realized that these people were at the center of a contemporary crisis in which their strength, their sense of justice, and their rights as human beings had been violated by a force beyond their own control. From that point on, I knew that men of this quality when aroused could not be put off with political answers which failed to reform the evils they faced. I saw many more parades in the next two years, some of them of members of the International Brigade which had returned from Spain, others in honor of King Edward VIII, others in welcome to Neville Chamberlain when he returned from Munich. I learned to discriminate among parades and to know that an older form of society represented by Edward VIII, Neville Chamberlain, and Daladier, had already broken up. I knew that there was a real struggle in which Hitler, Mussolini, and the nineteenth century friends whose sympathy they had won, were on the side of oppression and injustice, and that democratic movements among workers, intellectuals, poets, labor leaders, economists, and philosophers were on the other side. This did not appear to me at that time or since as a Marxist struggle of the classes, but as a struggle of many classes and social groups against fascism, military oppression, authoritarianism, and the police state.

After this kind of experience had been transposed into intellectual terms, I found new meaning in literature and philosophy. It seemed to me that the writers and philosophers of a current age were expressing through their work a set of ideas and basic assumptions about the society they lived in and the values of that society which they were concerned to foster. I had always assumed that the relation between literature and philosophy was one of intellectual influence and conceptual borrowing, and that the work of the scholar was to trace out the relationship between ideas and the concepts used to express a philosophical point of view. This, I assumed, could be summarized and set down as the philosophy of a period, an intellectual movement, or an "age."

I now decided that philosophers, poets, dramatists, and writers of all kinds were actually expressing something which underlay their own life in society, and of which most of the time they were unconscious. Just at this point I read Whitehead's *Science and the Modern World* and found in the fifth chapter of that book, "The Romantic Reaction," a statement of the way in which the relation between philosophy, literature, and society could be understood—a way which went far beyond the usual analytical scholarship to which I had grown accustomed. From that point on, I became interested in the conscious and unconscious assumptions made by philosophers and writers, and came to believe that the analysis of these assumptions was the first stage in understanding the meaning of a system of philosophy. This meant that I had become conscious of historical and social process, and I learned to see relationships between the economy, the politics, the philosophy, and the cultural values of periods and movements. I learned also that the disciplines which were identified as economics, anthropology, psychology, the humanities, and the natural sciences, and so on, were artificial devices used to define the limits of study and were in no sense real as actual divisions of knowledge.

As far as the study of philosophy was concerned, I also became interested in locating a given philosopher and his social and psychological setting. I asked the questions, "What, in the philosopher's experience, drew him toward certain problems rather than others?", and "What were the modes of experience which he was trying to explain through his philosophical discipline?"

This was an important part of any effort of my own to develop a philosophical position. I now had a means of comparison of my own approach to experience and to philosophical problems, with that of others. I found, in my work with students, that they, too, could be persuaded to consider themselves as embryonic philosophers who were looking for help in clarifying issues and problems which they could not understand if left to their own devices. The students and I could carry on a joint effort to obtain the answers to some of the questions which concerned us all.

This had the effect of turning my own thinking in the direction taken by William James. From Hume to James, by way of students, was to me a straight line, or rather, it was a curved line which went around the rationalists and dialectical philosophers of the nineteenth century, leading to James, Bergson, Whitehead, Santayana, and Dewey. I found in James the freshness of insight, the vigor of expression, and the freedom of intellectual movement which I admired as a teacher and as a beginning thinker. What attracted me in James was the direct way in which he cut through the concepts and apparatus of academic philosophy to the center of the whole philosophical puzzle, that is to say, to the immediate reality of individual consciousness. It seemed to me that everyone else had put things backward, that philosophers had reasoned from abstract principle to a stereotyped concept of the individual self. To me, James had shown that everything in the world was now relevant to the construction of philosophical concepts—the world within consciousness and known through consciousness was all the world there was, and one could live in the expectation that more and more fact and principle would become meaningful the more one gained through immediate experience. In practical terms, this meant a radical intellectual democracy, in which one could expect to learn from any experience, from any source, from any quarter.

What I had formerly conceived as a philosopher's world—the world of abstractions and concepts, of generalized experience expressed in categories—could now be seen as teeming with life, as if a microscope had suddenly revealed a complete new world of objects and living entities which were formerly invisible and therefore unknown. I began to see that one's openness to new experience was the first step on the way to clearer philosophical understanding, and that each new situation of consciousness was a new aspect of learning and of philosophy.

This way of looking at ideas was by now congenial to my own temperament. I had not dared to challenge the traditional attitude until I saw the example of James. I then read Santayana on James, and learned a good deal about what I thought by inwardly defending James against Santayana as I read. I learned even more about the areas of philosophy in which James and Santayana disagreed by the privilege of conversations with Professor Dickinson Miller, who described in vivid detail the life and mind of James and the relations which they bore to the work of Santayana.

I cite these items of intellectual autobiography to set a framework for describing a final discovery. This was the discovery of John Dewey. I had read John Dewey's books in the context of Whitehead, Russell, James, Bergson, and Santayana. I had found a greater strength in Dewey's position than in the others, and had come to feel that although Santayana, James, and Whitehead shared many of the same naturalistic convictions, it was in Dewey that these convictions were pressed to their ultimate meaning and thus yielded a greater variety of insights. But until I met Dewey I had not seen how serious a commitment one could make to philosophy, nor had I seen such honesty, clarity, range, and depth in any mind before. In meeting John Dewey for the first time, I discovered in him an example of selflessness, humility, and integrity which has served as an ideal ever since. I admire, respect, and cherish that image of a man committed to independent thought, to the discovery of new social ideas, to the use of ideas for human welfare, and to the defense of the individual mind against all forms of oppression. He gave to me, as he has to so many others, the sense of belonging to a tradition of humanism. The tradition, I learned, is shared equally by David Hume, by my friends the Welsh miners, by all those students, teachers, scholars, and individuals who show by their goodwill toward the intellect and the human race that they are committed to using the former for the benefit of the latter.

XII

ARNOLD TOYNBEE KINDLES A LIGHT

BY

DOUGLAS AUCHINCLOSS

The business of being a religion editor is a very funny thing—and I mean literally. There is something, I suppose, that is weird and anomalous about the combination of religion and journalism. It seems so at least to my journalistic colleagues; perhaps it is not so amusing to men of the cloth.

At a small club where I lunch once in a while, which is frequented by more journalists than clergymen, my peculiar calling is what they call in show business a running gag. It is always a surefire way of getting a laugh to announce, after introducing me to a stranger: "Mr. Auchincloss is the Religion Editor of *Time.*" People seem to assume that it is some kind of joke, that such a being does not really exist. As a matter of fact, it is such a good joke that last year it found its way into a hit play on Broadway—*Season in the Sun*. Apparently two of the characters (I was careful not to see the play myself) spend some time reminiscing about a girl named Agnes. "Whatever happened to Agnes?" one of them asks at last. Then comes the crusher that brings down the house: "She married the Religion Editor of *Time!*"

It is clear that a Religion Editor has to talk about either religion or editing. And since the "Moments of Discovery" that turn up in editing are rarely appropriate for such a gathering as this, religion it will have to be.

As a matter of fact, the religious side of my work has provided me with several "Moments of Discovery." And religion is not a bad thing to talk about either, because it has been getting to be something of a fashionable subject these days. You do not need a religion editor to tell you that the old girl has been getting quite a rush lately from the kind of intellectual highbrows who not so long ago patronized her like a country cousin, when they deigned to notice her at all. Today, more and more of them seem to be dating her, and it is common gossip that she is in an interesting condition.

By that I mean that there seems to be a sense of expectancy that something—perhaps a religious revival—is on the way. There is talk about larger and larger turnouts in churches and synagogues, about the prevalence of religious themes on the best-seller lists and the success of plays like *The Cocktail Party*. And judging by the amount of mail that comes into the Religion Section of *Time,* compared to the amount pulled by the other sections, there is something to all this.

Why? Whence this new lease on life for the religion so many people thought had been decently buried by Messrs. Darwin, Marx, and Freud? The answer, of course, depends on whether you happen to be inside a fold or outside—a sheep or a goat. Religion is on its way back, say the insiders, because man is at last growing humble in the face of his own pretensions. Western man's myth of inevitable progress and the efficacy of pure reason which took hold with the Renaissance, flourished in the Enlightenment, and triumphed in the nineteenth century, has at last exploded in his face. Wars, revolutions, economic and psychiatric breakdowns have shattered our illusion that we can go it alone, so we are coming back like the Prodigal Son to ask our Father's forgiveness. To the diehard outsiders—the goats—all this looks somewhat different. We are just plain scared, they say, and there are no atheists in foxholes.

Now you will notice that both the sheep theory and the goat theory have one thing in common: that any new surge of religion now under way is linked somehow to the parlous state of the world. And this brings me to what might be called a moment of discovery.

You all know, I am sure, the essay by Arnold J. Toynbee called "Christianity and Civilization." In it, he calls attention to the apparently antipodal relationship between religion and civilization. When civilizations are in their fullest flower, he says, their religions are in a state of corruption and decline. Contrariwise, spiritual life is at its most creative when things are going to hell in a hand basket. Professor Toynbee's conclusion is obvious: religion is basically at odds with civilization.

Looking back at the decline of the Roman Empire, the great historian, Gibbon, agreed. He saw the coming of Christianity as the calamity that sapped and weakened the noblest culture man had yet achieved and prepared it for easy conquest by the barbarians from the north. Of his *Decline and Fall* he wrote: "I have described the triumph of barbarism and religion."

This is certainly a very civilized point of view; to equate barbarism and religion as the twin enemies of all that is noble and good and beautiful. Is the City of God, then, really at war with the City of Man? Religious history does seem land-marked by attempts to resolve this enmity; the Roman Catholic Church is probably the most successful effort that is familiar to us all. But the kind of compromise between the Kingdom of God and the institutions of men which the Roman Catholic Church produces when it is least hampered by opposition—like Spain, for instance—does not impress many of us as very satisfactory, either from a temporal or spiritual point of view. Nor is this failure a peculiarly Catholic one. Whether the Protestants try it in Calvin's Geneva, or the Buddhists in Tibet, the results are depressingly the same. The Lord seems to have taken special pains not to expose his people, the Jews, to this temptation during the past couple of thousand years—even at the price of ostracism and persecution.

Professor Toynbee resolves the antithesis he poses by looking down on it from heaven. From that excellent vantage point, civilizations begin to look like handsome apples, ripening to red, juicy sweetness, but really existing only to rot and die for the sake of the seed inside.

Professor Toynbee puts it more poetically.

If religion is a chariot (he writes) it looks as if the wheels on which it mounts toward Heaven may be the periodic downfalls of civilization on Earth. It looks as if the movement of civilization may be cyclic and recurrent, while the movement of religion may be on a continuous upward line. The continuous upward movement of religion may be served and promoted by the cyclic movement of civilizations round the cycle of birth, death, birth.

. . . If, so far from its being the historical function of the higher religions to minister, as chrysalises, to the cyclic process of the reproduction of civilizations, it is the historical function of civilizations to serve, by their downfalls, as stepping-stones to a progressive process of the revelation of always deeper religious insight . . . then the societies of the species called civilizations will have fulfilled their function when once they have brought a mature higher religion to birth.[1]

This conception of the relationship between religion and civilization is, of course, a complete turning upside-down of all the premises and values commonly accepted by bus-riding, newspaper-reading laymen like myself. We assume, somehow, that religion is one of the adjuncts of a civilization, like good government or public education, and that it exists to make any given society a better place to live in. This is a logical extension of our assumption that religion is a device to make us better citizens, better fathers and mothers, and more generally decent to each other. But Professor Toynbee's line of thinking turns this right around. Morality, instead of an end in itself, becomes a byproduct of religion, as it were, and a country on the crest of power and prosperity is not necessarily being blessed by God at all. This idea that things are really at their worst when they are at their best, and at their best when they are at their worst, is a somewhat surprising and most uncivilized way of looking at the world. And it has some interesting implications for our time.

Everyone seems to agree that it is a dark time. A lot of us go on to say that what we need to get us through it is to return to the faith of our fathers. But if Professor Toynbee's insight is a true one, this hope is both wrong and impossible. Wrong, because we ought to be thinking about saving our souls rather than civilization. Impossible, because we can only move forward—albeit through shards and ruins—not into a faith-of-our-fathers' kind of time but into a religiously creative one, a time for new wine and the need for new wineskins. A time of prophets rather than priests.

[1] Arnold J. Toynbee, "Christianity and Civilization," *Civilization on Trial and Other Essays,* Oxford University Press, New York, 1948, pp. 235 f.

Prophets, of course, are very uncivilized. At best, they are unpredictable and embarrassing, like St. Francis taking off his clothes in the Assisi courtroom or George Fox trudging barefoot through Litchfield, bawling, "Woe to the bloody city of Litchfield!" At worst, prophets are downright subversive and have to be dealt with by the authorities. After the prophets have been dealt with, the priests take over. But it often takes generations of priests—or ministers, or rabbis—to civilize the messages of the prophets.

This, then, is another way of stating Professor Toynbee's tension between pure religion and civilization. And nowhere has it been epitomized so sharply and beautifully as by Dostoievski in the famous chapter of *The Brothers Karamazov* that is called "The Grand Inquisitor." You remember it tells the story of Christ's sudden reappearance in a little town in Spain during the Inquisition. Everyone in the town square recognizes him immediately and the people crowd around him on the cathedral steps. A funeral procession carrying the body of a young girl stops and sets the coffin down at his feet, and once again Christ raises his hand and pronounces the words: "Maiden arise." Suddenly, across the open square comes the Cardinal, the Grand Inquisitor, a withered, hawk-minded old man who had presided the day before over a brilliant *auto-da-fé* of Jews and infidels. At once he understands what has happened and beckons to his guard. The frightened people make way as the soldiers seize Jesus and hustle him off to a dungeon cell.

That night, the Inquisitor comes alone to the cell of Jesus. "Is it Thou? Thou?" the Cardinal asks fearfully, then adds at once, "Don't answer—be silent. . . . I know not . . . whether it is Thou or only a semblance of Him, but tomorrow I shall condemn Thee and burn Thee at the stake as the worst of heretics." From there on, the rest of the story is a monologue—for Jesus never says anything—in which the Cardinal defends himself and his Church.

He explains that he started out to follow Christ. But after a while, he came to see that Christ demanded too much of men. Jesus required of them that they be free. Whereas mankind—poor, weak, sinful, and pathetic as it is—did not want the dangerous stringencies of freedom, but wanted only to be led and fed and comforted. And so the Inquisitor, out of compassion, had turned from Christ and his cruel freedom to given men the authority and superstition and comfort for which they yearn.

Thus Dostoievski characteristically dramatized the conflict we have been discussing, between the pure religion of the saint and holy man and the corrupted, diluted compromise religion of civilized people like ourselves, who want, above all things, some way of eating our cake and having it. And Dostoievski, like Professor Toynbee, has tried, I think, to suggest a resolution of the conflict—not with a vision of chariot wheels rolling through the cycles of history, but in his own way, which is as personal and puzzling as life. Christ, you remember, says no word or reply to the Cardinal's harangue. But at the end, when the Cardinal is silent at last, Christ kisses him and disappears. That is all. What does it mean, that kiss? It is not given to us, or to Dostoievski, to know. But I am sure that here lies what hope we cake-eaters have. And if Professor Toynbee is right, our hope lies, too, in the sad disintegration of our world.

XIII

SOMETIMES A MIRACLE HAPPENS

W. G. CONSTABLE

When I was asked to address myself to the theme, "at that moment my imagination struck fire," I hesitated. Not being an artist, had I any imaginative powers to describe? And not being a psychologist, how could I describe them, if they existed? Second thoughts, however, have induced me to take the plunge. There is the flattery of being credited with an imagination; there is Emerson's remark that "Imagination is not the talent of some men but the health of every man"; and lastly, there is the hope that in a career which has included work as lawyer, soldier, painter, university teacher, and museum curator, at some point, like cheerfulness in philosophy, imagination might have broken in.

My first instinct was to turn to the lexicographers, and the dictionaries of quotations, to find out what imagination is. They were comforting but confusing—somewhat in the fashion of the divinity student who defined faith as "the capacity which enables us to believe that which we know not to be true." Johnson, for example, describes imagination as "Fancy; the power of forming ideal pictures; the power of representing things absent to one's self or others"; also as "Conception; image in the mind: idea"; and as "contrivance; scheme." Evidently, Johnson had in mind Francis Bacon's definition: "Imagination I understand to be the representation of an individual thought. Imagination is of three kinds; joined with belief of that which is to come; joined with memory of that which is past; and of things present, or as if they were present: for I comprehend in this imagination feigned and at pleasure, as if one should imagine such a man to be in the vestments of a Pope, or to have wings."

The comfort here was that I apparently possess imagination, because at the lowest I may claim to have conceptions and images in the mind, and to make contrivances and schemes—even to the extent of putting, say, an eminent rabbi into the vestments of the Pope. But confusion comes from the lexicographers seeming to put two things under the same heading; two things, related indeed, but different—Fancy and Imagination.

Fancy, I suggest, is primarily the rearrangement of facts, ideas, and concepts, to make a new pattern or arrangement, but from which nothing new emerges. Imagination, in contrast, I think of as making out of the material on which it works, a new whole; in other words, as being inevitably creative.

It follows from this that the products of the imagination, as distinct from those of fancy, have an internal coherence and unity—each part being inevitably and indissolubly connected with the whole, so that it is not possible to substitute something for that part, without changing the whole. In consequence, that which springs from the imagination must appear to its creator real and true, and have the powers to produce the same effect on a spectator or listener—though it may not always do so.

Fancy and Imagination differ also in the way they work. The one seems to be almost entirely an exercise of the conscious part of the mind, and to be mainly a matter of intellectual contrivance; the other seems to draw largely on the working of the unconscious. Only by making some such distinction can we, I think, understand the way in which the term, "imagination," has been used. It makes sense of the passage I have quoted from Bacon; and it seems to be implicit in Schiller's remark about imagination that "to one, it is the high and heavenly Goddess; to another, it is the competent cow that provides him with butter." I am not sure whether Johnson had the distinction in mind when he said that "all power of fancy over reason is a degree of insanity"; but I am tolerably sure that it was to fancy that Ruskin referred in speaking of "the faculty of degrading God's works which man calls imagination."

Wordsworth and Blake, however, seem to think of imagination as distinct from fancy when the one called it "the mightiest lever known to the moral world," and the other "the real and eternal World of which this Vegetable Universe is but a faint shadow." Indeed, we have come in ordinary usage to recognize the distinction, for recently the term, "creative imagination," has been coined to distinguish imagination proper from fancy. Let me quote some examples. Compare the inventions of Rube Goldberg or George Price with those of Signorelli at Orvieto or of Michelangelo in the Sistine Chapel. All these artists take the human figure as their main material; but with Goldberg and Price, it remains humanity as we know it rearranged into more or less fantastic or odd patterns; while with Signorelli and Michelangelo a new race comes to life, in a world distinct from ours.

Take another art, that of the novel, and compare Dreiser's *An American Tragedy* with Tolstoi's *War and Peace*. Both may be called realistic, for lack of a better term. Dreiser is mainly impressive by reason of the sheer weight of his accumulated facts and their skilful arrangement and never because his characters come to life; he is the newspaper reporter *in excelsis*. Tolstoi, in contrast, uses his facts to create a series of living people, whose personalities are more vivid than those of life itself, and move in ordered relation, one to another.

In these examples I have deliberately compared extreme cases. In each comparison, however, the artists in question are masters in their own spheres; and the very fact that they are so different emphasizes the distinction between fancy, which is largely conscious intellectual contrivance, and imagination, which lies behind power to create. But the line between the two cannot be drawn clearly and decisively at any particular point. The exercise of fancy may well merge into that of imagination, and in many cases the two may coexist. Indeed, I would go farther and suggest that fancy often provides the raw material on which imagination works, and that conscious contrivance may feed and stimulate the unconscious, and so breed imaginative activity.

Another point to be noted is that imagination is not necessarily directed to creation; it may also be the basis of sympathy and under-standing. This is not the place to discuss the theory of empathy; but certainly in the presence of any work of art, the realization of the whole, as distinct from the sum of its parts, calls for an imagina-tive act on the part of the spectator, the reader, or the listener.

So far, I have mainly had the arts in mind. The next question is whether imagination as I have tried to define it can find scope in any other field. There is, I think, no need to labor the answer. In the higher ranges of scientific thought, the solution of a problem is often reached before proof exists; in politics, an overriding concept or ideal may emerge before its constituent elements, or the means to realize it, have been thought out; and in the social sciences and humane studies, we are all familiar with the idea of a piece of work coming to mind, without precise scope and method being defined. One of the most famous cases is that recorded by Gibbon. In his autobiography he writes: "It was at Rome on the 15th of October, 1764, as I was musing amidst the ruins of the Capitol while the bare-footed friars were singing vespers in the Temple of Jupiter, that the idea of writing the decline and fall of the city first started to my mind." Then at the end of the book, he celebrates the realization of the idea.

I have presumed to mark the moment of conception; I shall now com-memorate the hour of my final deliverance. It was on the day, or rather night, of the 27th of June, 1787, between the hours of eleven and twelve, that I wrote the last lines of the last page, in a summer house in my gar-den. . . . I will not dissemble the first emotions of joy on the recovery of my freedom, and perhaps the establishment of my fame. But my pride was soon humbled, and a sober melancholy was spread over my mind, by the idea that I had taken an everlasting leave of an old and agreeable companion, and that whatsoever might be the future fate of my history, the life of the historian must be short and precarious.

This always seems to me an admirable example of the working of imagination. How great was the part it played in the writing of the *Decline and Fall,* can be best realized, perhaps, by comparing it with any German Ph.D. thesis.

So far, I have been speaking in generalities; now, my terms of reference bring me to the particular, where I must at times draw on my own experience. Even to try to analyze the imaginative process completely would be, for me, an impertinence. But observation, the writings of others, and my own experiences suggest some of the stages in that process. One of these is a sudden illumination, the birth of an idea or conception. I have already quoted one example, that of Gibbon; and I ought here to be able to add analogous examples from the visual arts. Here I am ashamed to say, knowledge fails me; partly, I think, because painters and their like, rarely bother to describe how their work came into being. One case, however, of which I was recently told, may be cited. The husband of a friend of mine was very anxious to have her portrait painted by Renoir. The couple went to see him, but he declined the commission firmly, on the ground that he was not a portrait painter. They noticed, however, that he was continually looking at the dress, of white satin, my friend was wearing. Finally, he suddenly changed his mind, and undertook to paint the portrait, provided she wore the same dress. What had fascinated him, and gave birth to the idea of a painting, was light falling on satin; and the whole conception of the portrait centered round this sudden visual impact.

Another example, this time in the field of art connoisseurship, is connected with Morelli, the Bergamasque whose methods of analyzing a work of art lie at the root of modern historical study. A famous *Reclining Venus* in the Dresden Gallery (now, we know not where, in Russia) had long baffled analytical methods; then as Morelli himself records, coming one morning suddenly upon the Venus "the spirit of Giorgione spoke to me out of the picture." This, from a man who consistently deprecated an emotional approach to works of art, and exalted the value of reason, is a notable example of sudden illumination. Whether in fact, Giorgione painted the Venus is now disputed, but Morelli's inspiration has been an accepted hypothesis for many years.

Such moments in my own experience have been rare but have occurred. The proximate causes were not always very exciting. One was the sight, as a boy, of a photograph of John Constable's *Cornfield* in the London National Gallery. From then onward I saw external nature in a new way—as a matter of light and air, of life and growth, in which all the elements sang together. The obvious results of that moment have been small—a few photographs and an occasional landscape painting; but had it not occurred, I might never have experienced such things as the haunting grandeur of the English fen country, and the glory of New York. Another example of a sudden new experience, came from reading, as an adolescent, Morris's *News from Nowhere,* and Ruskin's *Unto This Last.* Without conscious thought, the idea sprang almost full grown into my head that art was not a decoration of life, but an essential element in giving it dignity and purpose; and that idea has influenced and is still influencing my whole life. It will be noticed in both these experiences, there is a coming together into unity, the birth of something new, even if not original, which I think is truly the work of imagination.

But, these unheralded and unsolicited moments, are, in my experience, rare. Even when they seem accidental, it will generally be found they have been preceded by periods of brooding, contemplation, even of aimless experiment, perhaps not in the field where the imagination has worked, but in something related thereto. Often, however, they arise out of long periods of work on some task imposed by conscience or external authority, which is in the beginning nothing but a chore. Here, there is sometimes a conscious preparing of the way for the imagination. One more or less painfully assembles what seems to be relevant material—sketches, written notes, and so on, based on one's own ideas or culled from other people's work. Gradually these are built up into a kind of jig-saw puzzle, which has some kind of shape, but is in fact as dead as mutton. Many books, many buildings, many social and political schemes and theories never get beyond this point; and they remain dead, though like mutton, they may be very useful. But occasionally a miracle happens. The accumulated material begins to cease being a mechanical mixture and becomes a synthesis. In this the unconscious part of the mind seems to get to work. The whole takes shape, main themes emerge, details fall into their proper place, and the relevant is separated from the irrelevant. A familiar case which I myself have known is the solving of a mathematical problem in one's sleep. Of more interesting examples within my own experience, one is when I was painting from a model. The pose, from the point of view from which I was working, was difficult to realize; the lighting was tricky and was complicated by differences in the color of the skin. I had been laboring for two days, and was in a mess. I had analyzed this, thought about that, and tried everything; and the painting was still a matter of bits and pieces. Then, late in the afternoon, when I was tired and despairing, the brush began to move, almost, it seemed, of its own accord. Everything was seen simply and clearly, and the hand responded. In less than an hour, one of the few satisfactory nude studies I have ever made had come into existence.

Another example, in a very different field, had to do with the birth of an academic institution. I had for a long time been immersed in museum work, but had been asked to turn my mind to the problem of art history studies in the University of London. I well remember a long series of apparently barren speculations and inquiries which seemed to lead to nowhere. Yet hope remained, and one day, I think on top of a bus, the idea of the Courtauld Institute, which is the Department of Art History in the University of London, came into being, not only as an institution in itself, but as one organically related to the University; and on the idea born on that bus, the Institute is still based. At what point this miracle, as I have called it, may happen, there is apparently no knowing; though I have a suspicion that outside pressure—often in the shape of a deadline—plays its part. But that conscious invention and experiment—what I have ventured to call fancy—is the best breeding ground for imaginative action, I have little doubt. The *nulla die sine linea* of the writer may equally well be the ideal of the worker in the visual arts. This is not a recipe for success, but lays down a basic condition for imaginative achievement. The heart of the matter lies in a question and answer during the trial of the action brought by Whistler against Ruskin, arising out of Ruskin's criticism of Whistler's painting, *The Falling Rocket*. Cross-examining counsel asked, "The labor of two days, then, is that for what you ask two hundred guineas?" To which Whistler replied, "No; I ask it for the knowledge of a lifetime."

I well remember my friend and teacher, Wilson Steer, one of the best landscape painters of his time in England, going to his studio at nine o'clock every morning except Sunday and getting down to painting something. Only, he held, by painting all the time could you hope to seize the moment when imagination got to work. So it was with Walter Sickert, his contemporary, who would make a drawing of some selected subject, a painstaking record of every detail, such as the exact number of windows in a house, in his own special calligraphy; and from that make the painting in his studio. Only, he held, by working steadily on the facts and knowing them intimately could the mind eventually be set free for an imaginative use of them. Of the methods of work of older and greater artists we know less; but what we know points in the same direction. Take only one example, Rembrandt. On occasion a theme, generally from the Bible, would apparently strike his attention. He would then embody it in drawing after drawing, making experiment after experiment, until finally what he was trying to say crystallized, and a great work of art was born. It is interesting, also, in his case and that of other artists to see how the curve of their development moves up and down. A period of labor and experiment culminates in a few great works. Then new fields are explored, new methods tried, the results being more tentative and less convincing, until a new and richer synthesis is achieved, and a new group of masterpieces emerges.

Turn now to what happens after the moment of illumination when the imagination has come into action. There follows a period of dreary doubt, of intellectual questioning, of tests and trials. In this period, I suggest, it becomes known whether the moment of illumination was due to truly imaginative activity, with its creative implications, or was the result of fancy and contrivance—what we have come to call a "bright idea." Bright ideas can be very stimulating; but they rarely stand up under the strain of the period of disillusionment. Certainly, under that strain, imaginative concepts have also collapsed. One of the greatest difficulties in any piece of work in which imagination plays a part, is to keep the unity, the freshness of the original idea, while expanding and enriching it in the light of criticism, so that the structure of which it is the center of inspiration, becomes a living whole.

There is, I fear, little in all of this of comfort or help in these troubled times. Two things, perhaps, it suggests. One is that no first rate thing has ever been achieved in this world without imagination. Yet, "Unless the Lord build the house, they labor in vain that build it." And how are we to know whether what proceeds from that imagination makes for the good life or against it? But let us remember, "The wind bloweth where it listeth and thou hearest the sound thereof; but canst not tell whence it cometh and whither it goeth; so is every one that is born of the spirit." Of that spirit, I suggest imagination is one aspect, and that through it works the creative element in human beings.

A second point is that imaginative activity, though it may come unheralded and even as a surprise, has its roots in hard, unremitting work. Turner lying on the banks of a pond, and watching the ripples caused by stones thrown into it, would not seem to be one of the world's workers, yet on such intensive observations as these was based his vision of the sea, and his expression of its magic and might. So, let each man ply his trade faithfully; and sometimes perhaps, the clouds will open and he may see the City of God.

CONTRIBUTORS TO "MOMENTS OF PERSONAL DISCOVERY"

DOUGLAS AUCHINCLOSS, Religion Editor, *Time Magazine.*

LYMAN BRYSON, LL.D., L.H.D., Litt.D., Professor of Education, Teachers College, Columbia University; Member, Executive Committee, The Institute for Religious and Social Studies: First Vice President and Member, Board of Directors, Conference on Science, Philosophy and Religion; Author: *The Next America, Science and Freedom,* and others; Editor: *The Communication of Ideas;* Co-Editor: Symposia of Conference on Science, Philosophy and Religion.

W. G. CONSTABLE, M.A., *Cambridge University;* Curator of Paintings, Boston Museum of Fine Arts; Member, Board of Directors, Conference on Science, Philosophy and Religion; Author: *Venetian Paintings,* and others; Co-Author: *XVI and XVII Century Art in England* (with C. H. Collins Baker).

HARRY EMERSON FOSDICK, S.T.D., *Columbia University;* Minister Emeritus, The Riverside Church; Chairman, Executive Committee, The Institute for Religious and Social Studies; Author: *On Being Fit to Live With, The Man from Nazareth, Rufus Jones,* and others.

MORDECAI M. KAPLAN, M.A., *Columbia University,* Rabbi, D.H.L., *The Jewish Theological Seminary of America;* Professor of Philosophies of Religion, The Jewish Theological Seminary of America; Editor: *"The Reconstructionist";* Author: *Judaism in Transition, The Meaning of God in Modern Jewish Religion, The Future of the American Jew,* and others.

LAWRENCE S. KUBIE, M.D., *The Johns Hopkins University;* Clinical Professor of Psychiatry, School of Medicine, Yale University; Faculty, New York Psychoanalytic Institute; Committee on Psychiatry, National Research Council; Author: *Practical Aspects of Psychoanalysis.*

R. M. MACIVER, D.Phil., *Edinburgh University,* D. Litt., *Columbia University, Harvard University;* Lieber Professor Emeritus of Political Philosophy and Sociology, Columbia University; Member, Executive Committee, The Institute for Religious and Social Studies; Member,

Board of Directors, Conference on Science, Philosophy and Religion; Author: *Community—A Sociological Study, The Modern State, Society—Its Structure and Changes, Leviathan and the People, Social Causation, Toward an Abiding Peace, The Web of Government, The More Perfect Union;* Editor: *Group Relations and Group Antagonisms, Civilization and Group Relationships, Unity and Difference in American Life, Discrimination and National Welfare, Great Expressions of Human Rights, Conflict of Loyalties;* Co-Editor: Symposia of Conference on Science, Philosophy and Religion.

RICHARD McKEON, Ph.D., *Columbia University;* Distinguished Service Professor of Philosophy and Greek, The University of Chicago; Author: *The Philosophy of Spinoza, Freedom and History.*

MARGARET MEAD, Ph.D., *Columbia University;* Associate Curator of Ethnology, American Museum of Natural History; Author: *The Changing Culture of an Indian Tribe, Sex and Temperament in Three Primitive Societies, And Keep Your Powder Dry,* and others.

DOUGLAS MOORE, Mus.Dr., *Cincinnati Conservatory, University of Rochester;* MacDowell Professor of Music, Columbia University; Member, National Institute of Arts and Letters; Author: *Listening to Music, From Madrigal to Modern Music;* Composer: *Giants in the Earth,* and others.

JOSEPH M. PROSKAUER, LL.D., *Columbia University;* Chairman, New York State Crime Commission; Author: *A Segment of My Times.*

HARLOW SHAPLEY, Ph.D., *Princeton University,* etc.; Director, Harvard College Observatory; Co-chairman, Board of Directors, Conference on Science, Philosophy and Religion.

HAROLD TAYLOR, Ph.D., *University of London;* President, Sarah Lawrence College.

PAUL WEISS, Ph.D., *Harvard University;* Professor of Philosophy, Yale University; Author: *Nature and Man, Man's Freedom, Reality;* Co-Editor: *Collected Papers of Charles S. Peirce.*

INDEX

Abelard, Peter, 122
Academics, 120, 121
Action:
  and thought, 63-65
  and understanding, 73
Africa, South, 77, 81
Ages, characteristics of, 119, 120
Albertus Magnus, 122
Alexander the Great, 62-63, 120
Alexander of Hales, 122
American Federation of Labor, 77
American Jewish Committee, 76
American music, 2
American Tragedy, An, 153
"Angry Boy," 32-33
Anti-Catholicism, 76
Anti-intellectualism, 116, 117
Anti-semitism, 76, 95
  Zionist movement and, 96-97
Ants:
  Argentine, 21
  early, 20
  Harvester, 18-21
  species of, 19
Aquinas, Thomas, 108, 122
Arabic Aristotelianism, 122
Aristotle, 70, 74, 107, 108, 114,
  120ff.
Arnold, Matthew, quoted, 86-87
Art connoisseurship, 155-156
Art of Thought, The, 113
Artist, nature and value of, 1
Arts, American resistance to, 1
Associations, 71
At the Crossroads, 97
Auchincloss, Douglas, 145, 161
Augustine, Saint, 32, 108, 121, 126
Authoritarianism, 140
Autobiography, 83-84

Bacon, Francis, 151, 152
Bacon, Roger, 122
Barnum, P. T., 4-5, 13
Bastille Day, 95
Benedict, Ruth, 43
Benét, Stephen, 13
Bergson, Henri, 133, 141, 142
Bible, 95, 97
  commentary on, 96
Bigotry, 76, 81
Bill of Rights, International, 78
Biography, 83
Blake, William, on imagination, 153
Board meetings, 71
Boas, Franz, 43
Boethius, 121
Bonaventura, 122
Book, freedom from, 65-66
Boutroux, Étienne Émile Marie, 87
Boyer, Charles, 69
Brickner, Richard, 64
"Bright idea," 158
Brooks, Van Wyck, 2
Brothers Karamazov, The, 149
Browning, Robert, quoted, 39, 85, 88-89
"Bryan, Bryan, Bryan, Bryan," Vachel
  Lindsay, 5-12
Bryan, William Jennings, 5
Bryson, Lyman, 61, 161

Campanella, 123
Cassiodorus, 122
Catholic Church, Roman, 147
Catholic Welfare Organization, 78
Cepheid variable stars, 23-24
Chamberlain, Neville, 139
Charlemagne, 122
Charles the Bald, 122
Christian home, 85

"Christianity and Civilization," 146-148
Christianity, rise of, 107-108, 121
Church, organization of, 121
Cicero, 107, 113*ff.*, 118, 121, 124, 129
  rhetorical method of, 108
Cicero, Illinois, 81
Civilization:
  Jewish, 97, 99, 102
  and oral communication, 44-45
  religion and, 146*ff.*
Civilized industriousness, 64
Clarke, William Newton, 90
Class struggle, 138-139
Classes, theory of, 58
Clemens, Olivia Langdon, 2
Clemens, Samuel, 1, 2
Cocktail Party, The, 146
Coffin, *The Story of Liberty,* 38
Cohen, Morris R., 50-51, 53
Combinatory art, 127
Commission on Human Rights, 79, 81
Committee meetings, 71
Communication, oral, importance of, 44
Communities, organic, 102
Community relations, 96
Conferences, 71
Congress of Industrial Organizations, 78
Conscience, 88
Constable, John, 155
Constable, W. G., 151, 161
Contemplation, noble, retreat to, 74
Conversion, religious, 30, 31
Copernicus, 108
Cosmic truths, 59
Counter-Reformation, 123
Courtauld Institute, 157
Covenant of Human Rights, 81
Creative imagination, 153
Creative wonder, critical mind and, 52
Credit, desire for, 72-73
Critical mind, and creative wonder, 52
Criticism, higher, 96
Culture:
  Dewey's use of word, 112
  of primitive peoples, 43-44

Damaged personalities, 31
Darwin, Charles, 146

Death, war and, 67
Declaration of Human Rights, 81
Declaration of Independence, 76
Decline and Fall of the Roman Empire,
  The History of the, 83, 147, 154
Delta, star, 23
Democritus, 120
Demosthenes, 120
Descartes, René, 108, 136, 137
Detachment, extreme of, 69, 70
Devil, the, 31
"Devil and Daniel Webster, The," 13
Dewey, John, 108, 112, 118, 133, 142-
  143
Dialectical method, 125-129
Disciples, 61-62
Discovery, 105
  logic of, 106
  in philosophy, 106
Displaced persons, 67
"Don Juan in Hell," 69-70, 73-74
Dostoievski, Fëdor Mikhailovich, 149
Dreiser, Theodore, 153
Dumbarton Oaks proposals, 78, 79
Duns Scotus, 122, 126

Ehrlich, Arnold B., 96
Eichelberger, Clark M., 79
Elgar, Sir Edward, 14
Emerson, Ralph Waldo, 151
Empathy, 154
Energy:
  and thought, 62
  worship of, 63
Enlightenment, the, 146
Epicureans, 120, 121
Esthonia, 67-68
Ethics, and philosophy, 108
Evangelists, 86
Evasion of problems, 63
Existentialism, 49
Experimental method, 108

Faith of America, 102
Fame, desire for, 72-73
Fancy, and imagination, 152-153
Fascism, 140
Fauré, Gabriel Urbain, 14

Fosdick, Harry Emerson, 83, 161
Foster, Stephen, 1, 2
Fox, George, 149
France, 56
Francis, Saint, 149
Freedom:
  from book, 65-66
  from energy, 62-65
  isolation and, 68
  and menace of reputation, 70-72
  playfulness and caprice of, 74
Freedom of mind, 61*ff.*
  history and, 66-70
  internal chains on, 62
  worship of energy and, 63-65
Freud, Sigmund, 146
Friends, Society of, 29, 85, 87

Galaxies, 15-16, 22-26
Genius, and action, 64
Genocide, United Nations treaty against, 81
German Romanticism, 3, 13-14
Gibbon, Edward, 83, 147, 154, 155
Gibbs, Josiah Willard, 55
Gildersleeve, Virginia, 78
Glaspell, Susan, 42
God:
  as author of laws, 101
  conceptions of, 103
  as guardian of group spirit, 100-101
Goethe, Johann Wolfgang von, 69
Golden Bough, The, 43
Good, the, 115
Good Life, the, 33
  achievement of, 31-32
Gordian knot, 62-63, 65
Great Britain, and San Francisco Conference, 78
Green, William, 80

Haam, Ahad, 97
Hardwicke, Cedric, 69
Hartshorne, Charles, 54
Harvester ants, 18-21
Hebrew University, Jerusalem, 56-57
Hercules, star cluster in, 23, 24

Herzl, Theodore, 96
Higher criticism, 96
Historical semantics, 130, 131-132
Historical and social process, relationships between, 140
History:
  free mind and, 66-70
  war as, 67
History of the Decline and Fall of the Roman Empire, The, 83, 147, 154
History of English Literature, 134
Hitler, Adolf, 76, 77, 140
Hobbes, Thomas, 108
Hoeffding, Harald, 134
Holidays of Jews, 102
Holoscopic, meaning of, 129
Holy Ghost, 42
Home, Christian, 85
"Hound of Heaven, The," 88
Huckleberry Finn, 2
Hudson, Manley, quoted, 79-80
Human action, scientific method and, 129
Human behavior, science of, 108
Human nature, neurotic component in, 29
Human race, and human stature, 32
Human relationships, 28*ff.*
Human Rights:
  Commission on, 79, 81
  Declaration of, 77-80
Hume, David, 108, 123, 133, 136-137, 141, 143
  quoted, 135-136
Humility, 31

Imagination:
  creative, 153, 159
  Emerson on, 151
  fancy and, 152-153
  nature of, 151*ff.*
  and work, 159
Indifference, aware, 70
Individual, and proper name, 58-59
Individual ills, and social ills, 35
Industriousness, civilized, 64
Industry, genius and, 64
Inheritors, The, 42
Inhumanity, 75, 81

Inquiry, and speculation, 48
Intellect, and human race, 143
Intellectual movement, 140
Intellectuals, 38
International Bill of Human Rights, 77, 78
Intolerance, 76
Invitations, action against, 71
Isidore of Seville, 122
Isocrates, 120, 121
Isolation, freedom and, 68
Italy, 56

James, William, 30, 83, 133, 136, 141, 142
Jena, Battle of, 69
Jerusalem, Hebrew University in, 56-57
Jesus, in *The Brothers Karamazov,* 149-150
Jewish civilization, 97, 99
Jewish people, 147
    American, 102
    national holidays of, 102
    will-to-live of, 97, 98
Jewish religion, 99
Jewish Theological Seminary of America, The, 94
John of Salisbury, 122
Jones, Rufus M., 85
Judaism:
    and anti-semitism, 95-96
    as civilization, 97, 99, 102
    creation and creator, 98
    disintegration of, 97, 98
    meaning of term, 99
Justice, desire for, 72-73

Kant, Immanuel, 22, 108, 118, 133, 137
Kaplan, Mordecai M., 93, 161
Keats, John, 83
Knowledge:
    and action, 127-128
    philosophy as, 116
Kubie, Lawrence S., 27, 161

Language:
    creation of, 100
    forms of, 120

Language (*cont.*)
    and poetry, 14
Lanier, Sidney, quoted, 88
Laughton, Charles, 69
Lice, and history, 68
Lindsay, Vachel, 3-13, 14
    "Bryan, Bryan, Bryan, Bryan," 5-12
Lithuania, 94
Living creatively, 94
Locke, John, 108
Logistic method, 126-129
Longfellow, Henry Wadsworth, 39
Lost generation, 67
"Lost Leader, The," 39
Lovett, Sidney, 27

Machiavelli, 123
MacIver, R. M., 96, 161
Malinowski, Bronislaw, 43
Man:
    made in God's image, 60
    man's inhumanity to, 75
Man and Superman, 69
Marx, Karl, 146
Marxist class struggle, 140
Materialism, 87, 88
Mathematics, 105
McDowell, Edgar, 3
McHugh, Kate, 66
McKeon, Richard, 105, 162
Mead, Margaret, 37, 162
Melville, Herman, 13
Mental illnesses, 129
Meroscopic, meaning of, 129
Metagalaxy, 26
Method, schematic differences of, 130-131
Miami, Florida, 81
Military oppression, 140
Milky Way, 16, 22*ff.*
Mill, John Stuart, 106
Miracle, 151-159
Moby Dick, 13
Modern art and literature, 49
Money, lack of, 138
Moore, Douglas, 1, 162
Moorehead, Agnes, 69
Morality, byproduct of religion, 148

Morals, principles of, 108
Morelli, Domenico, 155
Morley, Lord, 72
Morris, William, 156
Moses, 93, 96
Munich, 139
Murray, Philip, 80
Music, 2-3
  denationalizing, 3, 14
  German, 3
Mussolini, Benito, 140
Mystery, 47
Mystery of Easter Island, The, 44
Myth in Primitive Psychology, 43

National Education Association, 78
Naturalism, 137
Neurosis, 27-36
Neurotic component in human nature, 29
News from Nowhere, 156
Newton, Sir Isaac, 108
Nicholas of Cusa, 116
Nizolius, 123
Nolde, O. Frederick, 79, 80
Nominalism, 136
Novelty, 105
Noyes, Alfred, 3

Ockham, William of, 123
Operational method, 126, 127, 129
Ophiuchus, 25
Oral communication, significance of, 44
Organic communities, 105
Original sin, issue of, 32
Otto, Max, 137-138

Painting, 3
  imagination and, 155-158
Parable of the talents, 41
Parker, Horatio, 3
Peace, Commission on the Organization of, 76-77
Peirce, Charles Saunders, 52, 54-55
Pentateuch, 93, 96
Peripatetics, 121

Personality:
  damaged, 31
  differences, 28
Persons, 47-55, 59
Philosophical semantics, 130, 131
Philosophies, four basic differences among, 118*ff.*
Philosophy:
  discovery in, 106
  as expression of cultures, 132
  as form of knowledge, 106-107
  nature of, 106-107
  as personal expression, 106, 110
  and religion, 84
  and scientific method, 108
  as social adjustment, 106, 110-111
Places, 55-57
Plato, 74, 108, 114, 115, 116, 118, 120, 121, 124, 126, 128, 129, 133, 136
Platonism, New, 121
Plodder, the, 64-65
Poetry, 1-14
  denationalizing, 14
  reading, 3
Polemo, 114
Police state, 140
Politics, science of, 108
Polynesians, 44
Primitive peoples, culture of, 43
Problematic method, 126, 127, 128
Problems, evasion of, 63
Prodicus of Ceos, 114
Progress, inevitable, 146
Promotion, 71-72
Prophets, 55, 148-149
Proskauer, Joseph M., 75, 162
Protagoras, 114
Protestant Council of Churches, 78
Proverbs, 48
Psychiatrists, 27
Psychiatry, basic premise of, 35
Psychologist, goal of, 30
Psychotherapy, 27-36
  as spectrum, 35
  successful, 30
Publicity, personal, 70-71

Quakers, 29, 85, 87

Radicals, 91
Ragtime, 2
Ramus, Petrus, 123
Realism, 136
Reason, pure, 146
Recognition, desire for, 72-73
Reformation, 123
Reger, Max, 14
Religion:
  and civilization, 146*ff.*
  by contagion, 85
  conversion, 30, 31
  differences among religions, 101, 104
  experience and doctrine, 89-90
  as individual experience, 100, 102-104
  Jewish, 99
  and liberalism, 90
  new insights, 105
  orthodoxy, 90
  sancta in religions, 101-102
  science and, 84, 86
  as social phenomenon, 100-102
  spiritual environment, 91
  static orthodoxies and, 91
  superstition and, 86
Renaissance, 146
Renoir, Pierre Auguste, 155
Reputation, menace of, 70-72
Responsibilities, sense of, 38
Revivals, religious, 86
Rhetoric, 108
Richer by Asia, 44-45
Roman Catholic Church, 147
Roman Empire, decline of, 83, 147, 154
Romanticism, German, 3, 13-14
Rome, as world center, 17
Routledge, Mrs. Scoresby, 44
Rubric dialectic, 125
Ruskin, John, 156, 157
  on imagination, 152
Russell, Bertrand, 136
Russell, Henry Norris, 17
Russian Jewish pale, 94
Russians, White, 67-68

Sabbath, Jewish, 94-95
Sagittarius, 25

Saints, 72
Sancta among religions, 101-102
San Francisco Conference, 77-80
Santayana, George, 141, 142
Schiller, on imagination, 152
Schoenberg, Arnold, 13-14
Scholastic method, 122
Scholastics, 136
Schools, relativism of, 116
Science:
  modern, 123
    beginnings of, 108
  of politics, 108
  and religion, 84, 86
  of values, 109
Science and the Modern World, 140
Scientific method, 108, 128-129
Scientific principles, new, 105
Scorpius, constellation, 25
Semantics:
  historical, 130, 131-132
  philosophical, 130, 131
Shapley, Harlow, 15, 162
Shaw, George Bernard, 69, 70, 73-74
Shotwell, James T., 76, 79, 80
Sickert, Walter, 158
Simonides, 114
Sin, original, 32
Skeptics, 120, 121
Smith, Al, 76
Social ills, 35
Social work, medical, 35
Socrates, 74, 114, 115, 128, 132
  and scientific method, 107
Sophists, 120
South Africa, 77, 81
Soviet Union, and San Francisco Conference, 78
Speculation, inquiry and, 48
Speusippus, 114
Spinoza, Baruch, 74, 108
Spiritual environment, 91
Spiritual experiences, 87
Stars, 15-16, 22-26
Steer, Wilson, 158
Steinberg, Milton, 50
Stettinius, Edward, 80

Stevenson, Robert Louis, 40-41, 134
Stoics, 114, 120
Stones, 58
Story of Liberty, The, 38
Streeter, Canon, 87
Success, 71
Sullivan, Louis, 55
Supernationalism, 81
Superstition, and religion, 86
Symbolic terms, 30
Symbols, 125

Talents, parable of, 41-42
Talmud, 95, 97
Taylor, Edward, 44-45
Taylor, Harold, 133, 162
Taylor, Jeremy, quoted, 90
Telencephalization, failure in, 63-65
Telesio, 123
Tennyson, Alfred Lord, 87
Theism, 86
Theology, 90-91
Theophrastus, 114
Theory, and practice, 127-128
Things, 57-59
Thompson, Francis, 88
Thought, energy and, 62-65
Time, 145, 146
Time scales, 18
Tolerance of intellectual differences, 131
Tolstoi, Count Leo Nikolaevich, 153
Torah, 96
Toynbee, Arnold J., 146
    quoted, 147-148
Trauma, individual, 37-38
Treasure Island, 134
Trivialities, practical, 70
Trotsky, Leon, 83-84
Truth, 116, 117-118
    cosmic, 59
    many ways to, 59
Turner, John Pickett, 49, 50
Turner, Joseph Mallord William, 159
Twain, Mark, 1, 2
Typhus, in Esthonia, 68

Unconscious, and imagination, 156-157

UNESCO, 113
United Nations:
    Charter, 78, 80
    Conference, 76
    and South Africa, 77
    treaty against genocide, 81
Universe, center of, 15
Unto This Last, 156

Values:
    philosophy as personal expression of, 106
    relativism of, 116, 117
    science of, 109
Varieties of Religious Experiences, The, 30
Veblen, Thorstein, 55
Vivas, Eliseo, 49

Wallas, Graham, 113
War:
    evils of, 67
    as history, 67
War and Peace, 153
Watts, Sir Isaac, 17
Webster, Daniel, 13
Weiss, Paul, 47, 162
Welsh miners, 139, 143
Wheeler, William Morton, 19
Whewell, William, 106
Whistler, James Abbott McNeill, 157
White, William Alanson, 34
White Russians, 67-68
Whitehead, Alfred North, 52-54, 116, 133, 140, 141
    philosophy of, 53-54
Whitehead, Mrs. Alfred North, 53
Whitman, Walt, 1-2, 3
Whole, and its parts, 124-125
Woodbridge, Frederick J. E., 111-112
Wordsworth, William, quoted, 87, 153
Work:
    doing one's share of, 68-69
    and free mind, 63-65
    hard, respect for, 64-65
    imaginative activity and, 159

World War I, 66-67
Worms, study of, 17
Wright, Thomas, 22
Wyclif, John, 38, 39, 42

Xenocrates, 114

Yeats, William Butler, 3
Yiddish, 94
Yudenitch army, 67

Zeno, 114
Zinsser, Hans, 68
Zionist movement, 96-97